ADVANCE PRAISE

"With masterful simplicity, Gene has created a selling model that finally brings together the essence of what other authors and experts have tried since the dawn of selling. The EDGE selling system focuses on exactly what sales professionals need to do to fully engage the buyer so there is no reason not to do business with you."

—FRANK TRADITI, HEAD OF SALES TRAINING,
ZOOM VIDEO COMMUNICATIONS

"I've had the pleasure of working with Gene in many capacities over the last twenty-five years. My appreciation for Gene's work lies in his honesty, integrity, and relentless passion to deliver sustainable results. He's one of the sharpest business leaders and has helped transform our company beyond our expectations. Gene is the real deal."

—CHAD BENSON, PRESIDENT AND CHIEF
OPERATING OFFICER, CBE COMPANIES

"We hired Gene and his team to create a winning sales strategy and help drive it forward. From day one, he delivered! He kept things organized and on track, and he did not let me waver from doing the same. His drive, leadership, and ability to get things done transformed our sales and marketing efforts, led to record-breaking growth, and laid a foundation that we have been able to carry forward. If you are looking for someone who can think strategically and provide the push you need to make things happen, Gene is your guy."

—JESSICA PARNELL, PRESIDENT, BRIDGEWAY ACADEMY

"During the transformation of our reactive sales force into a world-class systematic and proactive operation, Gene gave us the tools and momentum to achieve that in record time. Without him, it would have taken two to three years longer, and most likely we would have remained with lots of the typical blind spots for sales organisations, such as lack of a systematical follow-up process or training program."

—OTSO LAHTINEN, CEO, GEOBEAR EUROPE

"We had the pleasure to experience Gene in action during a complete week of a sales training for our complete sales team in Europe.

First, we did a two-day live sales training boot camp. This was a high-level, interactive training covering key sales topics, mindset, preparation, and focus. The ending session breaking wood was awesome.

Following the live session, we arranged biweekly calls for the sales team to strengthen their sales skills focusing on retention, acquisition, and development strategies and allowing them to develop their performance.

Parallel one-on-one webinars were arranged with the local sales managers, providing them valuable input to develop their interaction with their local sales team.

The whole sales training program was well prepared and very professional."

—NIELS-ERIK KONGSTE, VP SALES & MARKETING, AAF GERMANY

"Gene lives and breathes sales training. Whether on camera or in person, Gene conducts his training with professionalism and insight. Gene was able to understand the unique needs of our business and quickly develop a plan to execute. Gene's insight and sales knowledge are increasingly rare in today's business climate."

—ADRIAN VOORKAMP, DIRECTOR, SALES EFFECTIVENESS, GLOBAL FORTUNE 100 COMPANY

"It's not easy to get the trust of the person that you're selling to, but knowing and using the process of questioning AND listening to your clients and prospects is a proven means for understanding their needs and gaining their trust. Gene's skills in this area that gave him success as a salesperson and

sales leader, and the information detailed in this book can be applied to a salesperson's circumstances with immediate results."

"Working with Gene was not only a pleasure but also made a huge impact to my company's sales, market share, and ultimately the bottom line. The strategies that he teaches and uses made all the difference when it came to my company competing on a higher playing field with bigger players. Using his techniques gave my sales team the edge they needed to close more sales and maximize profits. Thanks, Gene, for your incredible work."

"Gene is one of the most charismatic and knowledgeable sales experts I have ever had the pleasure to meet. Gene intuitively understands people and how to communicate and connect with each individual. His enthusiasm and passion are infectious, and it motivates those around him to expect more of themselves and thereby achieve more."

"I had the pleasure of getting to see Gene in action a few years back. Today, I consider him a mentor. He lives and breathes sales, sales training, and motivation, and he is absolutely

the 100 percent real deal. I have carried what he taught me throughout my career, and today I am certain that I am more effective in my current role because of the time I spent learning from him. If you have the opportunity to bring Gene in to meet your sales force, you and your bottom line will be glad you did."

—KEVIN SORKIN, SALES DIRECTOR, BANKING INDUSTRY

"There are very few people who show up in your life as a good example, role model, and mentor—Gene is that person in my life. The wins that I have had over the last few years were a result of his leadership and coaching in my life. He understands the psychology and mechanics of running a business—particularly in the arena of sales management. He has contributed to the success of numerous people that I have worked with over the years. He is simply one of the best, highest-integrity, and most knowledgeable people I know."

—REGGIE BATTS, BUSINESS STRATEGIST

"I've known and worked with Gene McNaughton for over eight years, and this book is a compilation of the material that I've witnessed him teach to his consulting and coaching clients with incredible success. Gene is a master at breaking down the sales process into manageable morsels that you can easily understand and perfect on your own. Now you too have the incredible advantage of having years' worth of Gene's best content in one compelling book! I highly encourage anyone who wants to learn the secrets to successful selling in a sustainable fashion to not only read this book but to pass it on to others so that they can massively benefit as well. They will profoundly thank you!"

—JOE ROTH, ELITE CONSULTANT &
MASTER EXECUTIVE COACH

"I met Gene over twenty years ago. I quickly became a student of his and have learned much! This book contains the most powerful and useful ideas about selling. Whether you are trying to land that big deal or simply selling yourself for the big interview...this is your definitive Sales Edge! Thanks, Gene, for all the advice, mentoring, and help along my journey. You are truly an inspiration."

—CRAIG HOLTZEN, FINANCIAL ADVISOR, EDWARD JONES

"I've worked with Gene since our early days at Gateway 2000 over twenty-seven years ago. Gene's approach to designing a winning sales format for all types of sales roles has proven valuable in my career. We've used Gene for one-on-one and small groups, as well as company-wide sales strategies. I highly recommend engaging Gene to develop a sales strategy specific to your company's goals...you won't be disappointed."

—STEVE VAN GINKEL, VP OF PARTNER
ALLIANCE AND MARKETING

"Gene McNaughton is a master of sales who continually researches to discover how best to meet the needs and desires of buyers. Although I've been selling for over forty-nine years,

I never fail to learn from every conversation I have with Gene! He is one of my highly valued mentors. His new book The Sales EDGE is based on his years of sales experience and research. I've had the opportunity to preview the book, and I promise you it is a MUST addition to your sales library."

—HUGH LIDDLE, THE CHIROPRACTIC SALES
WIZARD, RED CAP SALES COACHING

"Over the years, I've had top thought leaders like Tony Robbins, Stephen Covey, and Tony Shea of Zappos at my events.

The best I know in the world of B2B sales training is Gene.

Read his book, implement his ideas, and truly learn how to close big deals. You will be glad you did. Gene has the best content out there—and he proves it every day. Just look at his client list."

—LARRY BENET, THE CONNECTOR

THE SALES EDGE

YOUR ULTIMATE GUIDE TO FINDING, KEEPING, AND GROWING ACCOUNTS

THE

SALES

E.D.G.E.

GENE McNAUGHTON

LIONCREST
PUBLISHING

THE SALES EDGE

Your Ultimate Guide to Finding, Keeping, and Growing Accounts

ISBN   978-1-5445-1148-1 *Paperback*
         978-1-5445-1147-4 *Ebook*

"The expert in anything was once a beginner."

*To my family, friends, co-workers, teachers, and
coaches who helped me get better.*

*To my kids Blake, Brady, and Gaby—who teach
me as much about life as I teach them*

I am grateful for all of you.

CONTENTS

ACKNOWLEDGMENTS

I am more than proud to say that I have received a ton of great coaching, training, encouragement, counsel, love, and support from many people. And I am thankful for the opportunity to recognize those people who have made such huge impacts on my life.

And, while this book took me over eight years to complete, all of you have inspired me to continue to write, despite being a busy sales leader, speaker, coach, and dad. And you have helped me in dealing with the ups and downs that life can offer.

If I thanked everyone, this would take twenty pages to write. If I missed you, then please know that I am forever grateful for you touching my life in a positive way. So many of you have encouraged me along the way, and in many cases, saw more in me and believed in me—even sometimes more than I believed in myself.

To my business partner and co-author, LaCosta Lolly. She has been my friend and business partner for more than seven years, and we have worked together for almost ten years. I like to tell people that clients come to our company for me, but they stay because of her. She is one of the most brilliant young marketing minds that you will ever meet. She is the COO and rock of our company, Growthsmart.

To my loving Mom and wise Dad (who are in heaven), and caring Mother-In-Law, Kathy Kirchner. You have always believed in me and been there during the great times and the most challenging times of my life. I am forever grateful for the encouragement and life lessons you have given me. Since my mother's passing, Kathy has become my new mom, and still sends me encouraging notes every single day. I am so grateful for her love and ongoing support.

To my sister Debbie, the most solid person in my life. Her love for me has always been unconditional, and I always strive to make her proud. She has been both my sister and best friend since I was a baby. I do not remember a week in my entire life that we haven't talked. She has been my biggest fan, supporter, and loving sister.

To my sisters, Susan and Lori. Your love, support, and

encouragement mean the world to me. I am so grateful that you are both in my life.

To my sisters, Cindy and Tina: I hope you are looking down from heaven with proud smiles on your faces. I miss you two every single day.

To the team at Book In A Box—specifically Robyn Burwell. This was the only company that I could find that could help get this book published, professionally, from its origin, to writing, and to final print. You have been the best partners I could have found for this important and challenging journey of writing an excellent book. I knew this would be a challenging task, and you were THE company to make it happen. I will be serving as your number one reference in the future.

To Matt Millen—THE greatest sales leader I have ever met. He has encouraged me to write this book for over ten years, and it was an honor for him to write the forward. This guy knows sales leadership better than any person I know. His track record is impeccable, and he always sees the good in every situation. He is my mentor and friend.

To my sports coaches in life:

- Gary Maxfield—the man who lead our little league team to a 21-0 final season and a city championship.

He was the first person to ever teach me about the power of intention. We did that and accomplished something big.

- To Dave Gomez who taught me about the power of PHD (Pride, Hustle, Desire) and the fact that NO foe is better than you, unless you think they are.
- Walt Fiegel—head football coach at East High school and the best motivator I have ever met. He led us to the State Football Championship in 1984, and is a legend in Iowa High School Football. He once said, "Never forget where you came from" and I will always honor those words.
- Jim Leavitt—my college football coach who taught me, regardless of how good I thought I was, that there was another level. I can still hear him today saying: "Buddy McNaughton, we gotta get you ready to play!!" Then, he made me do extra sprints and hill runs. He drove me harder than anyone in my life. While I may not have loved it at the time, he made me a better person. He was also the first person to make me write down my goals and hang them by my bed, so I would look at them every single day.

To my college professor and lifelong friend Pam Mickelson, from Morningside College. While in college, she was the person that encouraged me to study business and mass communications. What I didn't know at the time was that my life's work would be attributed to her wisdom, and gaining a great education at Morningside College. She was another person who saw more in me than I did myself, and I still stay in touch with her, twenty-seven years later.

To my early sales managers at Gateway, Todd Osborne and Star King. You helped me see what was possible as we built a multibillion-dollar company. You were also the people that encouraged me to move from sales management to sales training. You were the ones the encouraged me to build "The Ultimate Sales Playbook" and, with the help of others, we did. In fact, there is a picture of my first Sales Playbook later in this book. Because of them, I became a better seller, manager, leader, speaker, and trainer.

To Tony Robbins—my ultimate life mentor. For more than ten years, I've listened to your tapes and read your books. Then, I used what I learned to grow my career at Gateway. To be able to eventually work for you and get to know you was and is a lifelong dream. You truly walk your talk, and I will forever be grateful for you and your amazing wife, Sage.

To John Assaraf, who encouraged me to leave corporate America and carve my own trail. I will always grateful for you to "push me out of the nest of a base salary" and fly my own journey. You taught me more about Neuroscience and how to apply that to business more than anyone.

To the great Chet Holmes. Sometimes your hardest teachers are your best teachers. Chet taught me how to be a great consultant, salesperson, and speaker. He was never soft with words, but he knew that I needed someone super tough to be able to take my career to unlimited heights. I reference my learnings from Chet several times in this book. God rest his soul in heaven.

To my lifelong friends—

- Craig Holtzen—one of my best friends, who always encouraged me to be the best. His brotherly support will never be forgotten.
- Chad Benson—together we watched the movie "Wall Street" well over 100 times. We talked for hours about being successful. Now, Chad is the CEO of a +100-million-dollar company in Iowa. He is a great example that big dreams do come true.

To my life-long best friends: Brian Jepsen, Brian Daugherty, John Hofdahl, Brian Figge, Dan Thompson, Mike Sexton, Tom Schaff, and Brian Moses.

You guys know everything about me—and still like me!

I want to give very special recognition to Jennifer Shipman for all of her love and support as I was taking this book to the finish line. With her by my side, I achieved more progress on this book in five months than I did in the previous three years. The people we are around the most create a huge impact on what we do and don't do. She was my #1 cheerleader and held the fort down while I worked late nights to write and create. I am so grateful that this beautiful lady entered my life. Love you, Jenny Benny.

And finally, I am grateful for you, the reader of this book. I am thankful that you trusted me enough to buy this book and invest your time to read my teachings. This book is a compilation of the best of everything I have learned in over thirty-two years.

I hope that you use them to get powerful results for you and your company.

FOREWORD

BY MATT MILLEN

I love sales. I love both selling and being sold to. It's fun, as every sales interaction is fresh, unique, risky, and potentially lucrative. I have the highest respect for everyone who shares the love of the game, participates fully, and constantly prepares, practices, and trains to master this elusive art.

As a thirty-year sales enthusiast and a leader of high-performing sales organizations for over twenty years, I am both amazed by the amount of innovation and technology that is enabling today's modern seller, and I am shocked by the statistics around the performance of our collective teams:

- 50 percent of sales people will miss their number this year
- 65 percent of an average seller's day is spent on non-selling activity
- Most marketing leads are never followed up on
- The average tenure of a sales leader is under two years*

This is the result after the $20 billion-dollar annual investment U.S. companies make in sales training this year**.

And here we are, reading another book in search of unlocking and unleashing our inner potential and ability, in search of exceeding quota. You are most likely reading this book for the same reason I did; I am constantly investing in myself to keep learning, to keep growing, and to reinforce the selling basic principles that serve as a foundation of excellence. Gene brilliantly combines the mechanics and the mindset of sales, the two elements of success, in an easy to read and easy to utilize book of killer content.

I was given some timely advice early in my career: "It is better to be a 'learn it all' than a 'know it all.'"

This advice came at a time when I was very junior in my career and overly confident in my ability. In addition to advice, I was blessed to work for great leaders and had exposure to strong and caring mentors who chiseled off my rough edges, provided honest coaching and feedback, and didn't accept anything less than what I was capable of producing.

My mentors often saw more in me than I was able to see in myself.

Those individuals in your life are gifts; cherish them always.

Of the many mentors, leaders, and innovators we encounter throughout our sales careers, there are consistent attributes that separate the exceptional from the rest of the pack: impact and results. These individuals and their lessons, learnings, and systems stay with us, mold us, and shape our future. They make us better, they help us see things in a new way, and they push us far beyond what we thought possible and where we are comfortable.

The author of this book, Gene McNaughton, is one of those who has consistently delivered impact and results for himself, his co-workers, his friends, and his clients. As a friend, past co-worker, and active client of Gene, I speak from direct experience when I reference the impact and results Gene has had on my teams at Gateway Computer, T-Mobile, and now Outreach.io.

Gene and I have crossed paths over the last twenty years. He has helped my national sales organizations develop and grow as the sales landscape continues to evolve. I started selling in 1987, and there was little technology to aid the seller: no email, no internet, and no mobile as we know it today. What we did have were the three critical components to master in sales: telling the story, energetically and enthusiastically engaging in our sales activity, and creating and nurturing an unstoppable mindset.

Gene brilliantly and pragmatically blends the art and science of selling in a modern world. At the end of the day, selling is all about customer engagement requiring strong communication, presentation, and influence skills. *The Sales EDGE* delivers to the modern sales pro.

I will leave you with my favorite quote from Gene:

"You get rewarded in public for what you practice in private."

The fact that you are reading this right now says a lot about you. You are hungry for more. You are one of the few who DO, versus the many that talk. But don't just stop here. Read this book in its entirety. Have your entire team, those that work with you and for you, read this book. Have your peers and colleagues read this book. Take advantage of the many resources that Gene GIVES you in this book. And most importantly, know that what got you to where you are, will keep you where you are.

The only difference between where you are now and where you want to be are the intelligent actions you take from this day forward.

This book is the simplest, most well-written "playbook" to help you hunt, keep, and grow accounts.

Life is short, sell strong!

Matt Millen
SVP of Revenue Operations, Outreach.io
*Accenture and CSO insights
**Retrieve.com

PREFACE

I sat there. Stunned. In my basement-level home office. I had just listened to a voicemail from my boss—one I wouldn't have believed possible just a few months ago. But now? It was inevitable.

I had ninety days. *Ninety days* to turn it around or I was out.

Five months ago, I'd landed a promotion that put me among the elite top salespeople in the company. I was now a Field Corporate Account Executive.

With this new title, I thought I would hit the ground running, certain there was no way I could fail. There was NO company I couldn't win business from. I was coming to a new city, was going to pick up the phone, prospects were going to welcome me in with open arms, and the big deals were going to start closing quickly. It was a sure thing.

But that just didn't happen.

After five long months and hundreds of calls, I had zero promising leads, few meetings to speak of, and had given a handful of quotes that didn't convert to sales. Of the eleven Corporate Account Executives on the team, I was dead last. I knew it; everyone knew it. And it sucked.

I also knew I had to call my boss back—and that it was going to be an uncomfortable conversation, to say the least.

"Hey, Suzanne, this is Gene."

"Yeah...hi, Gene. Uhm...listen...we need to talk about your numbers. Yeah...it's been five months and...umm...we don't have anything on the...books yet. And, uh, your pipeline is pretty empty. And, umm..."

Her words came out slowly, pausing with each *umm*. A slight "tisk" sound clicked through the phone, like a mic picking up feedback. It literally was burning my ear on the phone.

She continued. "And, I need to let you know that, umm, if you don't turn it around in ninety days...umm, we're gonna have to make some decisions."

I sat there, listening to her drawn out ramble. I wasn't surprised at her words, yet it still felt surreal. My head dropped, my face sinking into the palms of my hands. How had I gotten here? Seven years I'd been with Gateway computers.

My mind immediately started walking through my long lists of blame—the reasons why my performance was suffering at this level: our brand isn't strong enough in the corporate space, our competitors have a dominating presence in the market, my targets aren't responsive and won't give me even two minutes to tell them what I can do.

I'd tried everything. Hounding gatekeepers to get a meeting with the boss, personally delivering gift baskets trying to get an "in" at the company, cold calling leads until I was told to quit calling so much. What more was there? It simply wasn't my fault.

I had to find a solution. Some way to get back on top and show Suzanne I was more than good enough—that I had what it took to be the best.

So, I started over. I went back to the very core of what I'd known from the time I was a teenager. My father used to tell me, "Anything it is you want to do, there's someone out there who's already done it. Buy their books, listen to them speak, watch them on TV, meet with others to learn what they know. Find people who are achieving what you want and do what they do—create your habits based off what successful people have done."

A FRAMEWORK EXISTS

The sales books I had bought but hadn't read yet, staring at me from a stack on my desk, suddenly looked appealing. One of them was Neil Rackham's *SPIN Selling* and the other was Anthony Parinello's *Selling to the VITO*.

I had nobody left on my list to call again, so I decided to take my dad's advice and start reading.

SPIN Selling taught me about the importance of asking specific questions in a specific order to understand their situation, problems, and priorities. I learned I had to identify the problems they had, and to *really listen*. By doing this I might be able to help them see the impact of their problems and build a need for my solution.

When I got to *Selling to VITO*, I realized I hadn't talked to a single decision maker, and that I had been meeting with and calling on people that didn't have the power to even make a decision. Heck, I had not even talked to someone that could *influence* the decision. I learned the importance of getting to VITO (the Very Important Top Officer). Back then, if *VITO* said the company needed something, then that is what the company did. VITO was the person who would decide what things would be and which partners or vendors they would work with.

In those days, you could cut a deal in the back room, or even the golf course if you were with the VITO, yet for most of the companies I'd been targeting, I couldn't even name that person.

Suddenly, I realized that I was targeting the wrong people, and now I had a different target. There were tangible steps in front of me. My spirits lifted, and I got to work. It wasn't the market's problem or the brand's problem or our company's problem. It was me. I was the chokehold to my company breaking into this market.

I was the person who, while working hard, was not working smart. Not yet, at least.

FINALLY GETTING IT RIGHT

Immediately, I started documenting. Where were my contacts—who was I talking to? What was happening with each account I'd been assigned?

The contacts I *did* have all loved me. It was easy to get in the door with them. I showed up with donuts or pizza, corporate pens or branded beer cozies, even Royals Baseball tickets. They'd always let me in because they knew they'd get something. The problem was, I never got anything in return. Not one of my contacts was a decision maker.

So, I shifted my contacts to a higher level, where I learned my next lesson: higher level people require a higher level of communication. Because this was back in the dark ages—back before email—I made calls and sent letters and did everything I could to get to the right people. Yet they all remained locked firmly behind the gatekeeper's door. The gatekeeper's job is to keep *you* away from *them*, and they're good at it. I had to be more disciplined and determined than ever.

I also had to face a deep-seated fear: Was I skilled enough to start calling those *VITO*s? Did I have the mental strength to make this work?

I'd never even attempted these people—presidents and CEOs of large, influential companies. I hadn't even identified them. But my job was on the line and the clock was ticking.

For a month, I built my database of decision makers (a robust Word document, really), and got to work. I befriended the gatekeepers. I took Anthony Parinello's words to heart and "used every means necessary" to get in the door.

A month of finally doing the right things after years of getting it wrong. And I still wasn't any closer to saving my job.

LUCK FAVORS THE PREPARED

Around that time, I slumped into our company's office after another failed attempt at one of the largest banks in the Midwest—the kind of organization that stadiums and parks are named after. On my way back to my desk, I ran into the general manager of our office. She stopped me cheerfully—her with friendly demeanor, high-end clothes, and a pristine Jaguar parked outside, and me with my shoulders stooped, head down, and job on the line.

"Hey, Gene! How's it going?"

"Good," I lied.

"Yeah, that doesn't sound like *good*. What's going on?"

"Ah, just struggling. I can't get to the people I need to talk to."

She said, "Well, is there any way I can help you?"

I half-sarcastically named the CEO of the bank I'd just left. *Ha ha, sure, you can help.*

To my complete shock, she said, "Oh, of course! I know

him. He's my neighbor. Just had him over for a barbecue the other night. Would you like to meet him?"

With a fast-paced walk, she went into her office. Five minutes later, she said, "Can you meet for lunch on Thursday?" She almost didn't get the last word out before I blurted, "Done!"

That was a Tuesday, and she secured me a lunch with him on Thursday. I had a meeting with the VITO. *Holy cow, here we go.*

I learned a powerful lesson in that moment. One that has shaped my career since that very moment: the answer to the unasked question is always "***no.***"

THE PROBLEM HE DIDN'T KNOW HE HAD

That was it. I was a total believer in everything I'd read. It had gotten me this far—I had a meeting. Granted, maybe I was just lucky, but who cares. I was going to do every single thing that I had learned from the books. For two days, I prepared like never before. I couldn't ask mundane and basic questions. Even if they can get to senior-level contacts, most salespeople aren't prepared to ask senior level questions. VITOs don't have time or patience for that.

Thursday afternoon, I rehearsed my key questions in

my head as I rode the elevator to the fifteenth floor of the bank's headquarters. Downstairs, on the main floor of headquarters, was the bank where I'd deposited my paycheck last Friday. But upstairs, all the way at the top, I was going to the executives-only floor to have lunch at the executives-only private restaurant with the CEO of the entire enterprise.

The CEO showed up right on time, ordered the cordials from a white-gloved waiter, and said, "Hi Sandra." Then he turned to me: "Kid, what can I do for ya?"

I'd never seen anything like it. I took a deep breath and dove right into my prepared questions.

We got right to the heart of it. The CEO told me he wanted their bank to be the technology envy of every bank in the world. I told him about a conversation I had with the teller who deposited my check that Friday, after I noticed her once-white desktop computer had aged into a dingy yellow.

"The computers aren't just old," she told me. "They crash all the time."

When I ran a few quick numbers for the CEO, I identified more than $250,000 in estimated losses across all branches thanks to these outdated computers, not to mention lost customers and damaged reputation.

Exactly twenty-nine minutes after we sat down, he ended the conversation: "Son, I'm done. This has been a productive meeting. Look for a phone call. My team will be in touch with you right away."

Two months into my ninety-day limit, I finally had a real conversation with a real VITO, and there was hope.

THE FRAMEWORK DELIVERS

I took the same questioning approach with the executives he told to call me. Because I had several meetings in the previous months with the front-line people, I knew their business well. I knew many of the challenges and frustrations they were dealing with. I also knew *VITO's* vision for the future. I provided roadmaps and solutions. I secured a trial shipment of ten systems, then showed up to watch their processes with new eyes, looking to identify pain points that we could eliminate. Their mundane routines—things everyone hated but hadn't even considered eliminating—provided opportunities for us to show them a better way.

We were able to provide systems pre-loaded with their bank proprietary software, cutting out the middle step that brought tech agents to headquarters to unbox, load software, and re-package, then ship the systems to their destination branch. It saved them hundreds of dollars per machine, freeing up the tech team to work on their existing tasks rather than tedious unboxing and loading of software. One month earlier, they didn't think they even had a problem. Until I showed them a better way.

When the phone rang with a Request for Proposal from that same company—they were taking bids for a complete technology refresh—I seized my clear opportunity:

"Hey, since that end-user shipping we've done saves so much time and money, wouldn't it make sense to include that as a requirement in the RFP?"

What I knew and they didn't was that none of my competitors could do that. I'd demonstrated such a valuable service that it had to be included, but it effectively locked everyone else out of the deal. If they were going to do this, they would have to have a third party load the software— thus increasing their pricing dramatically.

Just after the now-forgotten ninety-day "We might have to make a decision on your career" threshold, I had a 4,500-system deal on the books—one of the biggest in the history of our Corporate Sales division. Then I followed that same process with the area's largest insurance company. We did it again to make headway with one of the country's largest mobile phone providers at the time.

The Executive Vice President of B2B sales called me not long after that first deal. He congratulated me, then he asked me to spend the next six months documenting what I did and teaching everyone in the company to do the same thing.

After twenty years and billions of dollars of wins later (myself, my teams, and the companies I have consulted), that process has only improved. The book in your hands details my greatest experiences—wins and losses alike. It's the culmination of everything I've learned and refined to get from the lowest but greatest moments of my life to where I am today.

This book will detail, step by step, how you too can get *The Sales EDGE*.

INTRODUCTION

After interviewing and observing salespeople in action for the last 28 years, by this stage I would have to be pretty unintelligent to not see their common habits and patterns. In fact, it is extremely rare that I observe someone that has a clear and complete selling system. In fact, 99 percent of the sellers (and managers for that matter) are simply using skills that they have just "picked up along the way" of their selling careers.

With firsthand knowledge, my team and I see similar patterns in top performers, the middle, and the low performers too. Regardless of industry, country, or language, it is *always* the same. More importantly, this book will help you, wherever you rate yourself in the three categories above.

If you are looking to get even better, if you are looking to grow faster than ever before, if you are looking to shatter records—this book will show you, step by step, exactly what you need to do to hunt, win, and grow *the right* accounts; how to identify them, how to get in contact with the right people, how to run perfect meetings, how to get the right answers, how to present your solution with piercing effectiveness, how to move your deals forward. In addition, after you win, I will teach you how to keep those new accounts for a long time, how to grow them ("land them, then expand them"), and the *right way* to ask for and get referrals.

You need to know what to drop from your routine and incorporate habits and strategies that will help you connect with potential clients you never considered approaching and reach goals you've only dreamed of. Is this a sales pitch? No. I'm here to teach you how to be better than you knew you could and love what you do again.

THE IRRELEVANT SALESPERSON

With more access to information, communication, activity data, and forecasts than ever before, we, as business leaders, find ourselves under heavier, more profound pressures with every passing year. Access to such vast technology is working against us in many ways. While we are ultimately held accountable to drive revenue, margin, and profit, we are actually being pulled away from doing the MOST necessary activity—which is helping our sales teams excel.

As these technology "helps" continue to advance, we have more time-sucks pressing for our attention—twenty-four hours a day, seven days per week. I've been told more times than I can count that, "There's just not enough time in a week to get everything done." Sound familiar?

The buying process has changed. If you don't change with it, you could be in big trouble.

When do we finally say, "Enough is enough!"? When can we finally get to the point where we're able to focus our attention on *winning*, *keeping*, and *growing* accounts we've set our sights on? Let's face it, this **is** the only way to grow your business, and is what you are ultimately responsible for, right?

Whether you're the sales leader, the manager, or an individual producer, this book contains tools, strategies, and best practices that I've honed over twenty-eight years of field study to create massive success for my company and the companies our organization serves. I've built my professional reputation on a proven, documented ability to take sales teams, whether they are underperforming or not, and revamp their strategies, systems, and processes to ultimately turn them into top-performing, world-class sales organizations. I'm a sales organization fixer. *It's what I do.* And this book explains *exactly* how my team and I do it.

MY STORY IS YOUR STORY

As I write this, I am wondering: What really caused you to pick this book up? Are you a top performer who is looking for even more strategies? Are you someone who finally decided to stop reinventing the wheel, and you want proven step by step processes? Maybe you are the Sales Leader, and you want to get your entire team on the same page in terms of how to best hunt and win new business. Or maybe you're someone who just needs a boost. Someone that has been in a territory, and you are feeling a bit burnt out. You're finding that every quarter that you beat your number, you simply get a bigger number to hit next time.

Regardless of what got you here, I can promise you that you are in the right place. Spending money on a book is one thing. But spending money, actually reading the book, and then DOING new things—well, only the elite do that. But I can tell you, the elite **do JUST that**. It's way harder to find the three to four hours to read (or listen to) a book these days than it is to plop down a few bucks.

I have never met a top performer (in any area—sports,

theater, acting, etc) who wasn't constantly looking for the *EDGE*. Top performers constantly and consistently know that there is no ceiling when it comes to mastering their craft. They are constantly seeking counsel from coaches, teachers, trainers, and mentors.

I invite you to let this book serve as a gateway to helping you on your journey of creating sales mastery.

If you've read the Preface, you know I've been there myself. You may have even seen your own life in my experience. That's exactly why I'm writing this book. I want you have the playbook that will teach you the strategies and techniques I *wished* I would have known back then.

MY JOURNEY

My first steps into the sales profession were with Gateway 2000 computers. If you don't remember that company, it started as a dream in someone's barn and grew to a top-selling company that even outsold the giant in our industry. (Do you remember the cow spotted boxes?) In short, we like to say that Gateway went from "a barn to billions."

At the beginning of my twelve years with the company, I started off as a night shift phone salesperson, within eight months became one of the top performers, and soon worked my way into management. As the manager of the new hire Sales teams, I noticed that most of them, after a week of training, had NO idea on how to sell. So, once per week, instead of leaving at 5:00 for their dinner break, we brought our lunches in, and I started conducting sales training. I called it "The 7 Steps of Selling." After I would teach a class, I would then be able to listen to calls and provide on-the-spot coaching to each rep. Then, in a short time frame, we started to see drastic increases in our new hires being much more successful in a shorter period of time. My VP noticed this, and he, being a visionary leader and former athlete, was completely bought into the importance of training and practice. After seeing these breakthrough results, he asked me to start a newly created role as the Gateway Sales Training Leader. He asked me to document my coveted "7 Steps of Selling" process and to create and write the "Best Practices Sales Manual."

Then, instead of our new hire sellers just getting product training for five days, we shortened product training and gave them a FULL day of sales training. This included the "7 Steps," as well as language pattern training, persuasion techniques, and effective goal setting strategies.

Very soon, because everyone was consistently and effectively trained the right way, new hire performance flourished. In fact, it wasn't shocking to see new hire trainees out performing veteran salespeople.

Then the sales leader had another breakthrough idea. He used to say, "We need repetition! That is the only way to excellence!" So he had me go back and retrain the strategies and methodologies of the program on a daily basis.

It seemed the more we trained, the better we got. Every metric started improving, and improving at geometric levels. We quickly moved from being a "small business" to being a real player in the marketplace. Keep in mind, our products and pricing were still about the same, as compared to our competitors. It was our sales and marketing skills that caused us to literally EAT market share.

This was *the* sales training program which, over the course of the next several years, arguably created one of the most successful sales forces in history. We achieved this success in a tiny little town in a building in the middle of a carved-out cornfield in South Dakota.

Did we grow that fast because our products and services were spectacular and unique? I'm sure that was part of it, but definitely not all of it. We did have competitive products, but they soon became a commodity. The competitors we sold against had similar products and touted the same levels of service. We grew the business into a multi-billion-dollar company for one reason: we were a better sales and marketing organization. At our peak, we were generating more than $11 billion in revenue, with sales forces all over the world.

My next move was to go to work with the world-famous Tony Robbins, where I spent almost four years as the Robbins Research International's Global Vice President of Sales. We had ten sales teams in multiple states and countries selling events, products, and coaching services. I applied the exact same principles described above in my first thirty days there. We got clear on where we were, decided where we wanted to go, and built a plan to achieve those results. Under my leadership, that organization broke every record they'd had, at least twice—and in some cases, three times. We'd break a sales record, then we'd come back to set new goals. When we broke that record again, we'd start the process over. Keep in mind, this company had been in business for over twenty-nine years at the time. It was no small feat, and it was something that we're still proud of to this day. Again, we had the same products as before I arrived, but we geometrically grew the results due to better marketing and better selling methods.

I was then recruited to work with the world-famous Chet Holmes, author of the New York Times Best Selling book *The Ultimate Sales Machine*. At the time, Chet was known as one of the world's greatest marketing and sales consultants. Working side-by-side with Chet, he taught me how to be a great consultant. Together, we closed and managed the biggest consulting deal in the history of the organization. There are only a few sales consulting firms to have a single client pay them over $1 million in consulting fees. Together, Chet and I worked with a company out of Mexico, helping them grow from $900 million to over $1.7 billion (this is a documented fact, as they were publicly traded). Once again, same product, same pricing, same competitors.

The *only* things that changed were how they marketed, how they sold, and how they managed. That was the defining difference according to an interview with their CEO.

Since then, my team and I have consulted with over 100 companies around the world in multiple industries and sectors—from smaller companies with $1 million dollars in revenue, to highly technical equipment giants, from a Top 20 Accounting firm, to the largest provider of commercial security services in the world. We've worked with engineering firms, air filter providers, and even one of the "Big Four" wireless providers. We've worked with companies in more than eighteen different countries. While these companies seem quite different in their industry, geography, product, and service line, they share one common trait: the dedication to grow faster, smarter, and better.

There are a few areas that clients I've worked with, or who have studied my techniques, can attest to: I'm passionately and resiliently dedicated to mastering the selling process, I'm determined to out-distinguish the best techniques across industries, and I will vigorously perform those techniques at the highest levels myself, as well as teach others to do the same within their own organization. And let's not forget the importance of enjoying the process.

WHY YOU NEED TO *GET THE SALES EDGE*

In most cases, the divisions I've worked with, either as a business leader or a consultant, have either plateaued in sales or were seeing decreases in revenue and profit margins. In other cases, the business was doing well but the business leaders knew their sales team could and should be performing much better than they were. And in many cases, the companies that we've worked with are the premium price in their market, and under heavy price pressure. After working with more than 100 different sales division/companies in a wide array of countries, from a diverse range of industries and sizes, it's clear that sales organizations have similar patterns and issues keeping them from performing at their highest levels.

A UNIQUE TWIST

As I was writing this book, I had an epiphany. I thought, why don't I just call some of my friends that are now Directors, VPs, or Presidents of their companies and ask THEM what matters to them when dealing with salespeople? Why don't I just find out from them things like:

- Their perspective on what makes a good seller vs a bad seller.
- What causes some sellers to get through to you, and why?
- What do you want from a salesperson in the initial phases of conversation? What don't you want?
- What are some of your pet peeves relating to salespeople?
- What causes one salesperson to stand out from another?
- How do you make decisions?
- How important is lowest price?

Throughout the body of this book, you will see the comments, word for word, from people that you are calling on now. Once you hear what works and doesn't, you can adjust some of the techniques you are using to match up with what they want.

The most interesting part? What they want is exactly what you are holding in your hands—the information in this book.

ARE YOU REACTIVE OR PROACTIVE?

Companies that request our help usually fall into one of two categories. Group one is made up of companies whose sales have flattened, and they have competitors nipping at their heels trying to steal their accounts, usually with a lower priced offer. These organizations are struggling to keep clients, and they're looking for better processes and new ways to get and keep business.

Group two is made up of companies doing well but who know they could be doing even better. Their current success is often based on the strength of their product or service, but their leader (due to personal observations with their reps) knows they have a flawed selling process, or no defined process at all.

I recently had one CEO tell me, "I went on a sales call with one of our reps. He was like a talking website. He added no value, simply showed product information, and was totally reactive to the whims of the client. He had no control of the meeting. I had to jump in and take the meeting over. It was going nowhere, and it was embarrassing."

A smart sales/company leader knows that if they get their sales and marketing process to best practice levels, the sky is the limit for revenue, margin, and profit. And, like the first group mentioned, they're *always* looking for cutting-edge processes for winning new business.

A smart leader knows that he/she needs to be proactive at this, not reactive.

Here are some examples of a reactive environment vs a proactive environment:

REACTIVE IMPROVEMENT	PROACTIVE IMPROVEMENT
Suffering from flat/declining revenue, missing sales targets, profit erosion, and competitive pressure. Usually being driven to "make more calls" but often do not have a defined bullet proof process to do this well.	Knows their team and sales process has gaps but could perform better with better processes and training. Seeks out best in class employees, managers, and trainers. Is open to have an outside source of expertise to help speed up the process.
Struggles with (or does not have the time for) sales strategies, closing ratios, training, and processes to stay competitive and meet corporate goals. Is "too busy" to focus on sales training.	Commits to Sales Excellence by constantly improving in order to create record growth, proactively improve sales and profitability, develop team members, and create a legacy in the company. Knows that hiring and training people the right way is a key strategy to success.
Tries to understand gaps and areas for improvement, and attempts to take some actions improve, but lacks the time to dedicate to it. Because this person is in reactive mode, it becomes almost impossible to proactively create goals, train, and get the right tools into the hands of the sellers.	Is committed 100 percent to self and team growth/development. Understands their gaps and challenges, maintains what is working, and creates even better strategies for sales growth. This individual and his/her team are clear on their outcomes, strategies, and methodologies to create success. They have clearly defined what success looks like, and everyone in the organization knows too. They are constantly in self-improvement mode.

So, I'll ask you again: is your team reactive or proactive?

TAKE CONTROL AND DRIVE YOUR OWN EXCELLENCE

The truth is that *your* team can attain the high-achieving targets you envision. The strategies within these pages will help you assess problem areas within your group and get them using a playbook designed specifically for them. As we go, I'll act as your advocate, teaching you strategies I've learned over the past three decades and giving you the tools you need to grow your team's success. Yes, as each chapter progresses, there will be downloadable tools to help you guide yourself and/or your team. These are all for free.

Each chapter represents the techniques you need to give yourself and your team **The Sales EDGE**: getting your foot in the door in a new environment, knowing who and what to research, recognizing what's important to your targets, conducting prospect audits that will give you information no internet search could provide, creating and delivering your presentations, and maintaining your client base while growing your revenue from within. I'll teach you to use the *Sales EDGE* to push you into an abundance mindset of confidence and success that, when used with these techniques, will help you stand out from your competitors—both on and offline.

This book will help you develop deliberate practices and methods to teach your sales force "what great looks like" and to get them performing at their maximum potential. These are battle-tested processes that will give everyone on your team the ability be better than they ever imagined.

Prepare yourself, because you're about to make a paradigm shift that will put your career on the cutting EDGE toward success and growth.

Always remember:

The moment you think you know it all is the moment you start losing.

Now, let's get going.

PART ONE

MINDSET AND MESSAGING

CHAPTER 1

THE SEISMIC SHIFT OF B2B SALES

The world of B2B sales has never been more difficult or complex. Why? Because commoditization of just about every product and service type is increasing at a rapid pace. Internet service, contracting, cell phones, Google, social media, and video streaming services make access to information faster than ever before, and it is increasing at lightning speeds.

THE BUYING PROCESS NOW BEGINS *WITHOUT* YOU

Where consumers and businesses used to rely solely on sellers for their product and service information, the increased availability of internet research has made product information and pricing information easily accessible to potential buyers around the world. Whether your prospect is based in Cleveland, Sacramento, London, or Shanghai, with just a few clicks, they can learn anything they need to know before they even consider engaging a vendor or salesperson. In most business-to-business selling scenarios, prospective buyers will have already been to company websites, learned about products, studied spec sheets, read through pricing, and created a shortlist of providers they want to meet. Research proves that they're likely more than halfway through the decision process—before they even bring you in!

Then, if they are good, they will pit you against your competitor to drive down price: "We really like you, but your competitor is 20 percent less expensive. Now if you can match that, we will choose you." That's a common road to ongoing eroding margins and is not a path any of us want to be on.

Think about it—*every* dollar you give away in discounts cuts into any profit margin you will be getting. If you are a seller whose commissions are based on margin (and all compensation structures *should* be this way), you could be robbing yourself of income.

The accelerated rate of perceived commoditization, which we'll discuss more in later chapters, in virtually all industries has made it even more challenging to gain access to the people you need to meet with. Your access is becoming increasingly restricted because your website, your competitors' websites, and third-party resources are attempting (and, as you will see from the buyer's interviews, mandated) to do your job. If your company isn't on a buyer's short list, it's an uphill battle to even be able to have a conversation with the right people. In some cases, due to past experiences with pushy sales tactics, the people you're targeting would rather get a root canal than talk to a salesperson—at least until they absolutely must.

This is a monumental hurdle for you and your salespeople. It is the number one issue that every one of my clients struggles with. Based on historic human behavior, this "wave" is just the beginning.

OLD STRATEGIES, NEW BATTLEFIELD

If you think about it, the good old days seem really good now. Before the internet, buyers and procurement people would *have* to start their process by calling in salespeople, opening a dialogue, having multiple meetings, listening to pitches, and collecting research. It was only then that they would begin to narrow the field. If you were decent, you had a shot! Now, that's just not the case.

The taxing complexities of these shifting trends are the main reason salespeople are having increasing difficulty in landing mid- and large-sized accounts. Traditional (old-school) techniques have become less effective. In fact, as you will see in the client interviews placed throughout the book, companies whose sales teams apply these outdated, 1990s selling processes and sales techniques are seeing their sales decrease, margins decline, and long-term clients leave. Now, more than ever, it is an absolute imperative that, if you want to compete and win, you must adjust your selling messages, techniques, methods, and style to match the emerging trends of the new buying process.

If a salesperson falls back on the routine of selling on price, quality, and service, they'll soon be pushed into a commoditization situation where their only competitive difference is price. If you are the higher price, and you haven't convinced them of your competitive advantage, well—you know what will happen. It becomes a zero-sum game. Whoever can do the job for the cheapest price usually wins the deal.

THE "SAFER DECISION" MOVEMENT

Another challenge that salespeople face is the increased buying trend toward believing that "safer decisions are better decisions." Every company wants to reduce risk, especially when spending money. They bring *more* people into the decision process and make buying decisions by committee. There can be between five to eight decision makers in most mid- to large-sized opportunities. My firm's experience has shown this to be true with most of the clients we're consulting. One of our clients in the accounting/professional services business has faced situations where there were twelve people on a decision-making committee.

Today, nobody declares which solution to offer. We will have an entire team that needs to agree to the solution. In the old days, the CEO could say what needed to be done. It doesn't work that way today.

Think of this as a jury—there's obvious members of the jury:

- *CEO*
- *Technology expert*
- *Procurement*
- *The division leaders*
- *Other members of our Sr Team.*

The main point is that you MUST make sure you know everyone at the table. Not to get this is just plain naïve.

—BRAD R., PRESIDENT/PARTNER, BUSINESS PROCESS OUTSOURCING

The goal in these situations is to understand the committee's objective. The questions these decision voters must answer are simple: "Is the pain of our current situation greater than the perceived pain of change?" And, *if it is,* they ask, "Which company can we trust to give us the most *certainty* in eliminating that pain and helping us achieve our desired result?"

It's easy to understand the perception that safer is

better. Nobody is going to lose their job by making the safe decision. In business, however, anticipation of this decision-making mindset is power. We see this every day as we are quarterbacking deals for some of the largest companies in the world.

This is why your sales strategy, process, and pitch need to be sharper than ever.

Here's why decisions made by committee are so challenging. Each one of those decision makers has their own agenda, their own needs, their own priorities, and their own worldview. While the goal of the committee may be clear, each person is coming up with different answers to the questions they're asking:

- How can you help me and my company/division do what we need to do—and make me look good?
- Can I trust you to do what you say?
- How can you make my life easier?
- What makes you different?
- Can I see myself working with this person/team/company and enjoying it?

Procurement has an agenda of creating the most favorable pricing. Finance may have spreadsheets and long-term cost analysis. Each vice president/director must do what's best to achieve their divisional outcomes. The division manager, whose team will actually use your product or service every day, is likely understaffed and may not even want to change. *Their* concerns are entirely different:

- Does it work?
- Will it help me/my team do our jobs even better?
- Will this solution save us time?
- Will this solution help us get more done?
- Will this solution make my work life better?

The challenge is that, while all these different committee members have the same broad goal of solving problems and driving corporate growth, they usually have vastly different ideas of the best way to accomplish that. In some cases, they are overly concerned about how working with you may disrupt their lives. To win, you must be prepared to deal with multiple influencers who each have different agendas.

WHERE DOES THIS LEAVE YOU?

You obviously picked this book up for a reason. Somewhere in your mind you believe that you and/or your team could and *should* be selling at a higher level of effectiveness. But how do you find out the real truth?

Step back and think about your sales team for a minute. If an outsider, such as someone from my team, were to come to your office and request a one-on-one interview with five of your salespeople to discuss their selling processes and sales techniques, what would we hear? What responses would we get if my team role-played common selling scenarios like the following:

- We just met, and I asked about your company. How do you describe your company and what you do?
- You just called me, and I picked up the phone. What do you say?

- You just called me and got my voicemail. What would you say?
- What do you say on your second, third, and fourth voicemail? How often do you attempt a third or fourth voicemail? How many voicemails do you leave before you stop calling?
- We sit down for our scheduled meeting. What do you normally do or say?
- You are finally ready to deliver a proposal to me. How do you normally do that?
- Describe how you would respond to potential clients who say the following:
    - "We are in good shape with our existing provider."
    - "I need to think about it."
    - "Your price is higher than we planned to spend."
    - "Thanks, this has been helpful. We will get back to you."

Bad Voice Mails

Lousy voice mails: too fast, difficult to understand what it is they are saying. I have to hear and understand your name, and GO SLOW when leaving your phone number. Don't make it difficult. Articulation is EVERYTHING.

Mention your name at least twice, say your number, and repeat it. If I have to work for it, I am going to delete it.

Good voice Mails

Make sure and identify what you do, and WHO you do it for. Keep it short and to the point. If this is something that is hot on my plate, I might just decide to call you back.

—LARRY B., DIRECTOR OF TOOLS AND TECHNOLOGY

Now, would you be willing to bet that all responses will be similar and highly-effective? Would you hear something you're proud of? If your answer is "no" or "not even close," your team is literally flushing money and profit down the toilet. If this is the case, don't feel bad—you are in the same situation as 90 percent of *all* companies across the market.

Rather than just give you advice on how to do an internal

sales process audit, Chapter 4 will walk you through the steps to self-evaluate your team. Then, later in Chapter 4 you'll learn exactly how we perform an "audit" for the companies that hire us.

The road to the future does not look bright unless you adapt and develop a more strategic, modern set of sales processes and methodologies. In these pages, I'll walk you through every single step required to excel in today's B2B sales environment. If you've read through this chapter and seen a reflection of your experience in the words, you need to keep reading.

Your company's success depends on your willingness to make a change, and I can show you how to do that.

CHAPTER 2

SUCCESS BEGINS WITHIN

"Organizations are perfectly designed to achieve the results they're getting."

—TOM SEARCY, THE WHALE HUNTER

For decades, no human being had ever run a mile in under four minutes. It became a commonly accepted truth that is was simply impossible. It couldn't be done. Medical scientists even stated that the human body was anatomically incapable of accomplishing the feat, and anybody who came close would likely die from massive trauma to their heart. The entire world accepted this as a scientific truth; it was humanly impossible.

Then, in the 1950s, a young athlete named Roger Bannister made up his mind to run a four-minute mile. His coach told him it couldn't be done, but Bannister wasn't discouraged.

He visualized the time of 3:59:59 in his mind over and over until he convinced himself he could do it and committed himself to the extensive training it would take to accomplish his goal. He achieved this unprecedented physical feat on May 6, 1954, at Iffley Road Track in Oxford, England. His time was 3:59:40.

Just forty-six days later, after Roger Bannister proved it could be done, Australian runner John Landy broke Bannister's time by running a mile in 3:57:90. Science had been overruled, and people had recognized that it was indeed possible. Over the next few years, hundreds of runners broke through the four-minute mile mark; today, even high school students have achieved Bannister's dream.

Bannister created a new truth simply by convincing himself—by *believing* it was possible.

As soon as you stop believing something is impossible, it becomes possible.

MINDSET CHANGES EVERYTHING

When I'm brought in to work with a company, one of the first tasks is to assess the mindset of the team, including that of management and leadership. I always see a clear difference between an inspired, driven sales force and one that seems to be status quo, or even beaten down. Without exception, the inspired sales force believes they can shatter quota and break records. Nothing is impossible. And without exception, the team that is beaten down can't see past the quota wall they're up against. They've lost hope in being able to turn their struggle into success. This behavior isn't created because of a difference in products, market, or even skills; it's created by the leaders' methods and their mindset of success.

When I started working with Tony Robbins, I began to see and experience how important having an impeccable mindset really is. As I worked with and studied Tony's work, he inspired me to ask the same question over and over again: "What's the difference that makes the difference between top, average, and low performers?"

I wanted to understand what, specifically, top performers did differently. It became my mission to find the common traits and habits that make salespeople and sales organizations exceptional.

I soon realized there was more involved than just working harder. There was something there, something different in top performers—it was their mindset. That difference that made the difference was their mindset. My mission became to study and to learn, to be able to perform at that level myself, and, ultimately, to teach those same traits and habits to others in an easy-to-understand way.

That process drove me to study mindset mastery. I dove into the teachings of leaders like Deepak Chopra—who is the world-renowned expert on the connection of mind, body, and spirit—and thought leaders like John Assaraf and Wayne Dyer. Wayne famously said, "When you change the way you look at things, the things you look at change."

If you believe you can do something, that's the first step toward getting it done. But remember, there's a flip side to that truth: if you believe you *can't* do something, you'll never do it. You will find yourself getting in your own way and acting as your own downfall. Focus on the mindset that what you think about is what creates your truth, which will determine your actions and behaviors. What I have found is that the top performers in every field are the ones who are creating a better truth by training themselves to believe in their ability to succeed and to achieve exceptional results. That's the core power of mindset.

YOU ARE IN CONTROL OF YOUR THOUGHTS

It's been said that the human brain can have between 60,000 and 80,000 thoughts per day. The challenge is to control those thoughts and, more importantly, control the negative ones, which can consume upward of 80 percent of those thoughts. We all can have thoughts of self-doubt. Can I compete on this deal? Is the competition better than

I am? What if I lose this deal? What if this doesn't come through? This mindset can make the possible impossible.

Thoughts of self-doubt, uncertainty, fear, and anxiety (SUFA) are normal—they are the single biggest detriment to achieving and having what you want. The good news is, *you* are in control of your thoughts. Learning to master your response to new experiences, replacing those thoughts of doubt with thoughts of absolute belief is critical to overcoming challenges and achieving optimal outcomes. Sales teams that believe doubling sales is *impossible* won't try to—fear of failure and possible embarrassment will stand in their way. When those same people replace anxiety and fear with a belief that they are better than the competition and that those big deals can be won, not only will it become possible, it is the first step toward obtaining those achievements. Even if it takes an extra six months.

Every great salesperson and top performer has learned that their thoughts don't control them. They control their thoughts.

"Our doubts are traitors, and make us lose the good we oft might win, by fearing to attempt."
—WILLIAM SHAKESPEARE, "MEASURE FOR MEASURE"

Adding a fierce hunger for success to a proper mindset is the primary motivator for excelling in sales. If I'm hiring a new salesperson, I will always choose the one who's hungry. They must have that fire burning inside to achieve more. It's the same for sales managers, executives, and division leaders. You can hire the most experienced person who's been in the business for over twenty years—someone who knows the industry inside and out—but if they don't have the hunger it rarely works out. Hunger drives salespeople to learn new skills, new methods, to want to be the best, and to want to make the most money. Hunger is the central theme that separates top performers from the rest.

Know this: experience does not equate to effectiveness.

Charles Duhigg, author of *The Power of Habit*, found in his research that the importance of having a goal is made more relevant, clear, and meaningful when there is a greater purpose behind that goal. This "why" may vary for each person. It represents motivation and purpose. For someone whose "why" is feeding their family, avoiding debt, or avoiding the loss of their livelihood, hunger can be an overwhelming presence. For those whose motivation is to keep their title or clock in every day—it's a different story.

I can always tell the hungry salespeople vs. the ones that are going through the motions.

Hungry people follow up to my requests, and quickly.

If you are not being responsive and are too slow in getting back to me, you are out. Or if it takes too many calls to get to the actual core of the matter, I will dismiss you.

—LARRY B., DIRECTOR OF TOOLS AND TECHNOLOGY

Hungry people are the ones who stand out, not just in sales, but in leadership, in sports, and in any profession. The salespeople who are the hungriest for success are always the ones at the top. As a leader, then, it is your duty to lead by example and encourage your sales teams to be unified, engaged, and committed to the larger outcome. Focus on the meaning and purpose of your work and how it benefits your clients, your team, their families, their career, and their income. Focus your team around the greater purpose of solving challenges for as many customers as possible.

THE POWER OF ENVIRONMENT

If you want to do more, make more, and grow within an organization, you have to be around other people who share that drive. You pick up habits and behaviors from those you are around the most, so you've got to be very smart about your peer group. If you're surrounding yourself with people who aren't hungry and who are living in a constant state of complacency, or even complaining, you're going to find yourself mirroring and emulating those behaviors. However, if your peers are achieving great things and seeing the "glass half full," then you will be more likely to do the same. Bottom line: if you want to be a rock star—immerse yourself in the presence of other rock stars.

Surround yourself with allies, not liabilities.

THE MASSIVE ACHIEVEMENT MINDSET

High performing salespeople set their baseline by asking the question, "What can I be doing *even better*, and who and where can I learn to do that?" They believe any achievements that've been done before can not only be met, but also be beaten.

When I first start working with a new client company, the first thing I tell them we need to work on is establishing a Massive Achievement Mindset instead of a status quo mindset. I'm often surprised at the response executives give me: "Hey Gene, we don't really need the mindset training, we're pretty good at that. We just need the marketing tools, we need the strategy, we need the selling skills." I always have to challenge them on that. I say, "I agree that you need the tools and the strategy and the skills, but none of it matters unless we instill a mindset of absolute success. Then we will give them the tools to succeed."

I have to get the entire team, from the top down, thinking bigger. They have to believe that breaking records, shattering expectations, dominating the industry, and out-selling top competitors is a real possibility. That's where it all starts—with mindset. And it seems the bigger the company, the more likely there's an entrenched status quo mindset. Often this is the most important work I do.

Reset the bar, define the next level, build the plan, and execute like crazy.

ESTABLISHING NEW TRUTHS

There's a difference between truth and belief. A truth could be, "We've never closed a million-dollar deal before." But if you let that truth become a consistent belief, a consistent way of thinking, you will *never* close a million-dollar deal.

Think about the Robert Bannister story: the truth was that no one had ever broken that four-minute mark. That truth created a belief, even within scientists, that it couldn't be done. Yet Bannister's belief was that it could be done. He trained and pushed himself until his belief became his truth. You can do the same.

Winning beliefs come from establishing *new* truths. This mindset creates an enhanced way of thinking. Then those thoughts create belief. Those beliefs create actions. And those actions create new truths. Believing that you can close million-dollar deals will lead to the actions necessary to make it happen.

The Massive Achievement Mindset starts with the leader of an organization, then it resonates to management and is edified at the sales rep level. You must have a leader who has an extraordinary mindset because that is where the rate of the pack is determined. If that leader doesn't have the mindset, then it's not going to show up on the front lines either.

LEADING ABUNDANT SUCCESS

I remember when Ted Waitt, the Founder of Gateway Computers, addressed the sales team in 1992. He called an "all hands on deck" sales meeting. I remember seeing him standing on a chair, drinking a coke, and smoking a cigarette. With his sunglasses on and his hair in a pony tail, he declared, "One day—one day, we will sell more computers than IBM." At that time, IBM was one of the biggest companies in the world. They were certainly the biggest in the computer industry. Gateway was just a tiny speck of dust compared to IBM. I distinctly remember being in that room with sixty other sales people, and a whole bunch of them chuckling and saying, "This guy's crazy."

But Ted had the power of a Massive Achievement Mindset. I looked in his eyes, I heard the conviction in his voice, and I saw the certainty he had. He was absolutely convinced it would happen. And in just a few short years, Ted's dream for Gateway became truth, and Gateway sold more computers than IBM. In fact, IBM eventually stepped out of the computer business. There is no way this would have happened without a visionary leader standing up and declaring his belief.

I can tell you, it changed my life. I realized that the only thing standing between achieving our goals is how we think, matched up with relentless execution. This guy truly believed that tiny little Gateway Computers in North Sioux City, South Dakota would beat the behemoth IBM. Today, Ted Waitt is regarded as one of the most brilliant business leaders of his time. He was just a kid from Iowa with big aspirations, and he got a team to believe in them. That's what your job is, as a leader.

HABITS OF TOP PERFORMERS

Top performing sales reps have six essential habits that

set them apart from average performers. All of these are habits that you and your team can emulate. The key is to develop all six as daily, consistent habits that eventually become second nature, so you never forget to do them.

HABIT ONE: GET CLEAR ABOUT WHAT YOU WANT THE END RESULT TO BE

Top companies determine in the beginning of the year what exactly they want to accomplish. Top performers decide at the beginning of every year how much money they intend to make that year. They begin every day knowing what the outcome of that day and every meeting will be. They begin every week, every month, and every quarter with a clear picture of how it's going to end. They focus on a series of predetermined outcomes. There is immense power in clear intentions, because in many cases you may find a faster route to the outcome.

HABIT TWO: BELIEVE IN THE POWER OF CERTAINTY

There's a visible difference between a genuine intent to serve their clients versus their intent to sell and get a commission. When you commit to achieving your objective—figuring out how to serve people at the highest level—you gain confidence in your product and your ability to provide your clients with the best service. You become determined to serve others, and that determination will become part of your mindset. That internalized commitment will be visible in your actions, your conversations, and presentations. Confidence and enthusiasm are contagious.

HABIT THREE: ABP (ALWAYS BE PROSPECTING)— *BUILD* YOUR SALES PIPELINE BEFORE IT IS EMPTY

As Harvey Mackay famously once said, "Dig your well before you're thirsty." Top performers don't sit around hoping and praying that their two or three big deals come through. They are consistently and routinely prospecting, developing new business, and looking for ways to expand existing business. They're always building up their contacts and their pipeline, and "digging that well." There are going to be times when deals don't close, or deals get pushed. If you're relying on one or two deals to make your number, you're taking a big risk. Top performers have a pipeline that is bolstered on the front end by continually reaching out and being proactive. This involves using all tools, including the phone, email, networking, and social media.

HABIT FOUR: DO YOUR HOMEWORK AND ALWAYS BE PREPARED

Imagine going to an interview not knowing anything

about the company you've applied to work for. Perhaps you didn't look at the job description or find out what you would be doing. When the interview questions start hitting you and you have no answers, you've proven that you have minimal interest in the company, in the work, and in making sure you can have a conversation about what you can bring to the position and the organization.

With as much information as we can get online within seconds, there's simply no excuse for not taking the time to find out who you're meeting with, what their company is about, and getting to know more about their market-place. Prove to your prospective clients that you are one step ahead and offer a beneficial relationship to their company and their life.

HABIT FIVE: KNOW YOUR COMPETITION

If you're clear about who your competition is and know their products and how they sell, then you can counteract their strategy. You can anticipate what sales message they're going to deliver to your prospect. Here is a great example:

"YOU'RE NOT COMPETING AGAINST A HUGE COMPANY"

When competing against a big, dominant company, or any competitive company for that matter, you must realize that you're not competing against a huge, global brand. You're not competing against their fifty years of history. You're not competing against their thousands of employees worldwide. It's not David versus Goliath. It's just your team of two to four people versus their team of two to four people. That's it.

Once you realize this, it helps you to reframe your mindset and approach. You don't have to beat their entire company, you just have to beat a few of their people who are going after that same deal.

Years ago, when my company was fairly small and new, we were working with a multi-million-dollar security company on several small projects. The work had gone well, and they were happy with the results we were helping them get. One day, a large contract came available and my company was invited to submit a bid. We were thrilled that we were even invited!

About a month after submitting our bid—one of their senior people, whom I'd developed great rapport with during our time working with the company—called me to tell me we'd been selected as one of two final companies for the contract.

We were excited, to say the least, but somewhat intimidated. Our competition was *the* largest consulting company in the world. How were we, a small company, going to compete with one of the biggest consulting companies in the world?

It was at that moment that my contact told me, "Gene, remember, you're not competing against the company, you're competing against their sales team."

Those words changed everything. I knew our team could beat their team. We knew we could out present, out prepare, and out strategize their three or four salespeople. We knew our stuff and knew we knew the company better. It changed our entire approach and our enthusiasm to win that Whale Account.

And I'll tell you what, we won that contract. It was the first time we'd signed with a larger company, and within five years all our contracts were with large-scale organizations.

That one comment had changed everything for us. Remember, as it relates to competition, it's you and your team versus them and their team.

HABIT SIX: CONDUCT POSTMORTEM REVIEWS

Great sellers already know the road ahead—the steps in the sales process, how they're going to win. They know the best sequences to follow. When the sale is done, they have the mental strength to step back and say, "What really went well in that deal?" But they also have the ability to say, "What could have gone better? What could we have done differently?" Winners take the time to go through postmortem reviews. When a deal goes sideways, they are able to take these same steps. They're able to look back, take responsibility for their actions, and to recognize what they did wrong. They own it. This is the very definition of metacognition, a concept we'll discuss later in the chapters of this book.

MASTERING YOUR BRAIN

Do you ever wonder where your thoughts come from? First, keep in mind that you are in total control. After countless books, seminars, and personal coaching sessions, I've boiled this subject down to three simple pieces. If you can work toward mastery on these three topics, you will see your results soar.

KEY #1: THE PSYCHO CYBERNETIC MECHANISM

Our brains work kind of like the thermostat in your home. If you set the thermostat at 72 degrees, the heater or air conditioner will kick on, but once it gets to 72 degrees it will turn off. The brain works the same way. These are called our standards. The standards you set for your life determine how you live. This is called psycho-cybernetic mechanism (PCM).

Where you set your financial thermostat is likely where your hard work will get you, but rarely above it. To achieve more, you must set your target at a level that strives for that larger goal. Set a goal of doubling your income year over year. Set that high target for yourself, then believe you can reach it. That will determine your behaviors, your habits, and your daily work ethic. Your intention is everything.

You won't overachieve the standards you set for yourself.

One of my mentors, Chet Holmes, helped me understand this in a way that I never had. He talked about earning "life-changing income." This was a mental challenge for me. Up to that point, I was progressing financially, making an average of about 10 percent or more each year. I thought I was doing well, until he fiercely challenged my thinking and my standards.

He told me, "Don't just think *about* life-changing income, think *from* it." Think from the place of already having achieved your goal. What will you do now that you've doubled your income? Will you pay off some bills, buy a new house, upgrade your car, put more money toward investments, send your kids to college?

In fact, he forced me to set a goal of *doubling* my income. At first, I thought it was impossible. But I wrote it down. I put my goals on my wall, so I would see them daily. I had pictures of things I wanted to buy (a car, a watch, vacations, etc.).

That year, that's *exactly* what I did. I doubled my income—and it all started by changing my mindset and raising my standards.

Jim Rohn said, "If you want more you have to become more." Set your targets high in all areas, then strive to become the person required to achieve them.

KEY #2: NEUROPLASTICITY AND WHAT IT MEANS TO YOU

Here's a comment I hear more than you'd think: "Well, Gene, I've been doing this for a long time, and well, um, you know that you can't teach an old dog new tricks."

When I hear this statement—and I often do—I always remind them of the concept of neuroplasticity. "Neuro" means brain, and "plasticity" means flexible. The human brain has incredible potential to expand, learn new skills, and adopt new ways of thinking, regardless of age. I will often ask audiences: "How many languages can a child learn?" Once they think about it, they say, "Unlimited." Which is true.

The truth is that the brain never gets "full." There's no cap on how much information you can hold. Your brain maintains an elasticity which allows it to grow and stretch.

Any one of us can learn anything we set our minds to: learning a second or third language, playing chess, mastering social media, and definitely learning new sales skills. The main prerequisite is that there must be desire. If you decide you want to learn, your brain has the capacity to do it, no problem. You own the power to learn and change. Do you want to become an even better leader or a better manager? Do you want to become a higher producing sales person with a corresponding income? The proven truth is that the prerequisite to learning is first committing to the act of learning and clarifying why that is important to you. But to say that your brain is full is pure fantasy.

The moment you think you know it all is the moment you start losing.

So, when it comes to the sales techniques contained in this book, it's not about whether or not you can do this, but are you willing to? Do you have the hunger? What I ask is that as you read this book, don't let your mind be the guardian of what's possible for you. Don't let what you've done in the past set the bar for what you can do in the future. You are about to take a quantum leap in your sales success. Believe you can do it, and the coming pages will be your guide.

KEY #3: UNDERSTANDING YOUR RETICULAR ACTIVATING SYSTEM (RAS)

This is the part of the brain that is in control of what you think about and what you notice. The brain tends to focus on six to seven thoughts or pieces of information at a time. For example, when you notice or focus on something wrong, you tend to start seeing and hearing more about that wrong and noticing it more in your surroundings. What you focus on, you tend to attract more of.

Consider this: have you ever bought something, like a car—and suddenly you see that car everywhere, where you hadn't really noticed it before? Your brain notices and spends time on what you're thinking about the most. Where your focus goes, your energy will flow.

The good news is that you are truly in control of this.

This is why goal setting is so important. It's all about visualizing yourself succeeding. Focusing your brain on specific and intentional thoughts causes it to spend more time there in order to make it a reality. Athletic teams hire psychology coaches to work with their athletes to help them with visualization and meditation—seeing themselves over and over again in their perfect performance. Standing on that podium receiving medals.

This strategy works in your life and career in the same way. Goal setting and visualization are incredibly powerful tools in guiding your success.

THE CAUSE-EFFECT RELATIONSHIP OF SUCCESS

I want to challenge you to not just rely on goal setting. We all know how to set goals, but you may be surprised to learn that less than 10 percent of people actually *do* set goals.

Let's look at it from a new perspective, one that helps you see beyond that goal line. When you're establishing your goals, start thinking about your success in terms of outcomes.

What I like about outcome-based thinking is that you can establish desired outcomes for anything just by asking yourself a simple question: "What is the outcome I want from this action or situation?" Every meeting should start with determining the desired outcome. If I go into a meeting and find that no agenda has been set, I can start by asking the group or the meeting leader, "What's the intended outcome of this meeting? What do we want to achieve?" It's that simple, and it can apply to anything—a conference, a presentation, or even today, this week, or this year.

Setting an outcome allows you to get clear on what needs to happen. You can and should establish desired outcomes in every area of life and business. It allows you to take a proactive approach, to clarify what you want, to plan how to achieve it, and then constantly adjust your plan to gain success.

Again, in two years, you *will* arrive somewhere. Don't just drift through life. Set your targets in every area—your business, your income, your body, your relationships— even for physical things that you want to have. You will be happily surprised at how much you can achieve simply by setting clear intentions.

When I look back on everything I am most proud of in my career, I realize that I (accidentally at first) followed the principles that I laid out above. Here's a great example. As my consulting career was taking off, I became fascinated with watches. I was working with increasingly successful people and noticed almost all of them had really nice watches, usually Rolex. When I started looking into Rolex, I had no idea how expensive these things were, but I wanted one and I was going to have it. So, I decided to test the power of outcome-based thinking.

At that time, I was working with Chet Holmes, author of the book *The Ultimate Sales Machine*. I was the president of Chet's consulting division. Chet always preached to me that real success was not about achieving small, incremental gains in income. He said true success comes from focusing on life-changing income. Chet was always driving me to do more, have more, and become more. He was such a powerful force in my life.

One year, he challenged me to reach an incredibly high-revenue goal. I said, "I'll commit to that number and, when I achieve it, you have to buy me a Rolex watch. This is the watch that I picked out." It was the Rolex Submariner with a black face, the one that I saw in a magazine and was determined to earn.

For that entire year I had a picture of that Rolex taped to my computer screen, next to my phone, and hanging on the wall at home. I looked at it every single day. I had a plan in place to achieve that number, and I knew that in twelve months I would do whatever it would take to achieve it. I just kept focusing on, "What do I need to do to reach my number?"

I got to the last month, and it was down to the wire. I needed to have a huge month and had to get all my clients to pay before the end of that month. I remember scrambling when a client said, "Look, we're not going to be able to wire the money until the first day of the next month." I called the CEO at the airport and told him we had to have it in that day. When he said, "It can't be done," my focus became apparent to me. My mindset was focused on achieving my goal and "can't" became just a word, not an obstacle.

I asked, "Who else can we call? Can we call the CFO?" I knew that this one extra deal would get me over that huge number. In my mind it was going to happen; I was not taking no for an answer. Sure enough, we got the deal and the money wire. That day!

I literally doubled my income that year. I served more clients than ever before. I look back on it and I think, "Was that the law of attraction? Did I set the big goal and focus on it exclusively? Did my brain help me find new opportunities, make more follow up calls, get on more stages, and have more tenacity in going after those accounts?" I believe the unequivocal answer is yes. I have followed that same process in every area of my life since then, and you can too.

WHERE WILL YOU BE IN A YEAR?

So, in the next twelve months, you're going to end up somewhere. Where you arrive depends on what you focus on—your aim. Just like driving a boat, if we don't aim toward a specific point, we drift. There's immense power in declaring in advance where you want to end up twelve months from now, and then focus on getting there. A boat that has a definite destination may get blown off course, it may even take on water, but it will soon get back on course and arrive at its destination.

In my experience, our lives are just like these boats: without clear aim, we can drift. Don't just be a drifter—set your target in advance, knowing that we completely underestimate what we can do in the course of twelve months or more.

CHAPTER 3

OUR PROCESS, YOUR WAY TO SUCCESS

"See your business as it is. See your business better than it is. Then build a plan to achieve it."

—UNKNOWN

It happens every time. When our team goes into a company to perform an audit, we find that the individuals within the same organization and even the same peer group are doing things differently.

Though all of them are selling the same product or service, the sales process usually varies from person to person. When we interview five or more salespeople at the same company, we will get no less than (you guessed it) five or more different descriptions of their sales process. There is rarely consistency in the sales process or the selling strategy between them.

And that is costing companies dearly.

Based on this overwhelming fact, you can understand why I say that most sellers execute their profession based on "skills they've picked up along the way." While the new salesperson you hired shows three to ten years of sales experience on their resume, I find myself asking the same question every time: "Who trained them?" Have they been through formal training that included the basics: consultative selling methods and solution selling methods? My years in the industry tell me that for most people, the answer is no.

Here's the bottom line: you should be selling at peak levels (as long as you have a relatively competitive product), but likely from top to bottom, you know you aren't. And let's face it, if every company could sell at the highest levels—with consistent, well-thought-through techniques—they would be. If it were easy, you'd be doing it.

That's exactly what my life, and this book, is all about—helping you create consistency, peak performance, and more profitability in your company. Later, in Chapter 7, we'll get into the specifics of the EDGE. But it starts by getting real with yourself. Not rose-colored glasses real; I am talking about committing to owning every single result you are getting. The key is to be honest and self-aware.

What I find is that, whether you are a seller or the business leader, when you own the current results, then you step into owning the future.

YOUR FIRST STEP: AUDIT YOUR ORGANIZATION

When my team goes into an organization on a consulting engagement, the first thing we do is perform an intense sales, marketing, and customer service audit. We look at everything within their current processes to understand what is currently happening in an organization that drives revenues and gross margins. After reviewing all metric details, trending reports, financials, training, processes, and procedures, we use the information as a gauge to understand everything that is being done to create the results that this client is achieving. Mind you, we are not as concerned with the actual results. We are more concerned with understanding exactly what is happening to create those results (revenue and profit are the ultimate scoreboards) that they are getting.

Then, the deep dive takes place. We interview members of the team at every level—from leadership and management, to marketing, sales personnel, operations, customer service, and administration—all with the design to learn what they do to create current results. And, we give each interviewee complete confidentiality.

Our job is to know the truth: what is working, what is not working. What is preventing you/your company from selling at peak levels? What are some of the inefficient processes that need to be reevaluated, or, what should be in place that isn't? We find that the front-line folks, the people who are dealing with day-to-day customer engagement are the ones who *really* understand the circumstances a company faces.

Our objective is to uncover every issue, every problem, every roadblock, every organizational bad habit, and every gap in the process, so that we can figure out what needs to change, and in what order, to achieve peak performance and take them from their current state to their desired state of growth and profitability.

As a reminder, if you decide to do this yourself, it's critical that you give each team member complete immunity and confidentiality. It's much harder to gain honest information from employees when they feel they're under threat of losing their job or embarrassing themselves in front of their peers. This is often why it is better to have a third party conduct the audit.

As a *great* leader, you *want* this feedback, don't you?

Typically, we ask each person to walk through their average day, discuss their processes, and talk about their strategies and performance. We want to understand their systems, from how they prospect and gain access to new accounts to how they decide which accounts are worth spending more of their time on. Digging deeper, we explore how they run their meetings, build and present proposals, handle objections, and, subsequently, how they follow up.

> If you, or a third party conducted interviews with your sales-people, would you/they hear a consistent, persuasive, and highly effective approach across the board?
>
> If the answer is *no*, you are leaving profit on the table.

Next, we gain meticulous clarity on where the company needs to be and by when. This is primarily based on revenue, profits, new market share, or comparisons/rankings vs. their competitors. The best companies in the world operate on two- to five-year plans. Weak ones don't have a plan. You would be surprised by how many companies we go into where the sales people don't even know their targets. How can someone hit a target that has not been established and agreed upon?

Finally, we configure a strategy for what needs to be changed, added, or removed to create the roadmap for them to achieve their optimal results.

Once we determine the company's growth plan, we go to work integrating the agreed-upon growth strategies at every level of the organization. Growing at a fast pace is not easy. It requires everyone in the organization to participate and commit to creating massive results.

Ideas are a dime a dozen. Execution is what causes results.

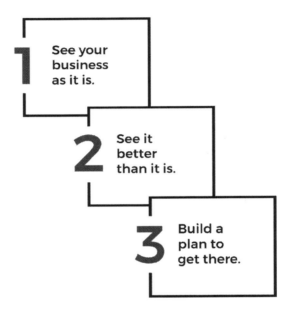

1 See your business as it is.

2 See it better than it is.

3 Build a plan to get there.

PRESENTING OUR FINDINGS

When the audit is complete, one of the best ways to present findings is in a group setting. We conduct an executive briefing with all the stakeholders (including sales, marketing, customer service, engineers, operations, and all management) in one room. We then hold a private leadership meeting for the comprehensive strategy and action plan.

In the executive briefing, we do something rather unexpected. Instead of presenting fifty to seventy PowerPoint slides to tell them everything we found, we start by engaging the team in an interactive discussion to increase their own awareness of their strengths and weaknesses. This is accomplished through (1) a true/false test and (2) ten telltale responses no leader wants to hear.

1. SUCCESS IS BINARY: TRUE OR FALSE

The first portion of the presentation is called the Group True-False Test. This consists of ten questions, which creatively identify key issues holding a company or team back from achieving peak performance. We ask the entire group these questions, reading them out loud, and request that the group respond verbally to each one by saying either "true" or "false."

Try taking your own True-False Test. Read the questions and respond to each one honestly, based on your organization. If you're really committed and want to go through this process with your own team, pull them into a room and ask them these same questions:

GROUP TRUE-FALSE TEST

	TRUE	FALSE
We have clear, written processes and selling systems in place. Everyone on the team understands, uses, and executes these at high levels.	☐	☐
We have a clear roadmap for sales and sales growth. Everyone knows and understands the strategy and their role in executing the tactical details.	☐	☐
We have consistent and highly effective sales strategy trainings and we practice with Yoda-style mastery.	☐	☐
Each person could easily and readily recite our best practice sales process highlights for every phase of our sales cycles.	☐	☐
We implement ideas with precision and accountability until they are completed. We don't skip from idea to idea.	☐	☐
Each person on our team could easily, consistently, and persuasively answer the question, "What makes you different than your top two to three competitors?"	☐	☐
We have a library of case studies, and we have have a system for sharing our "big wins."	☐	☐
We are confident and highly persuasive in handling our top three to four pre-identified objections. In fact, it is rare that we rely on discounting to win deals.	☐	☐
We have multiple proactive strategies for getting in front of clients. We are clear on who we should be contacting and utilize multiple tools to schedule meetings.	☐	☐
We have outstanding marketing "collateral" (online and offline marketing tools) that support our sales team, to gain access to decision makers, run highly effective meetings, and present our proposals with piercing effectiveness.	☐	☐
Our sales managers know their numbers, run fantastic and regular sales meetings, and effectively observe and coach their reps on a one-to-one basis.	☐	☐

Remember, this process is about being real with yourself and asking your team to do the same. Did you answer the questions honestly? If yes, good.

Now, let's examine the results. If you answered "true" to more than seven of the questions, then your sales organization is far ahead of the 100+ companies we've worked with. In fact, if this is *really* true, you may be among the absolute best-of-the-best in the world.

But, if you're being completely honest, it's unlikely that you answered "true" to more than a few, which means the *truth is*: you're leaving money on the table. Every question you responded "false" to can and does tie directly to your ultimate revenue and profit performance. Most companies we interview answer "false" to almost all these questions. This reality may be uncomfortable, but I invite you to see beyond the discomfort and recognize the abundant opportunity you can be tapping into.

2. TEN TELLTALE COMMENTS

During the second portion of our presentation, we read a collection of quotes gathered during the interviews. This concept represents a fantastic strategy I learned from Chet Holmes, author of *The Ultimate Sales Machine*. The interview quotes are taken directly from conversations with the employees and read word-for-word to the entire group. We lovingly titled the list, "Quotes I Wouldn't Want to Hear if I Were CEO."

Of course, we keep the individuals' names confidential and never reveal who said what. The quotes illustrate key findings and speak volumes to the problems and challenges within the organization. When we hear comments like these, we know exactly what needs to change and can prioritize our strategy based on the goals of the company.

After doing sales audits for the past decade, we've heard some truly remarkable comments—even some rather embarrassing ones. However, it's interesting how consistent the responses are from company to company.

I've pulled together some examples for you to read through. These are actual quotes we've heard during sales audits we've performed.

> I've been told what's expected of me, which is to make calls, but have gotten no training on how to get in front of people. **Nothing works. I call, I email, and I get no response.** Out of 100 calls, I might get one callback.

> I can't explain what the current sales process is. We all do things a little differently. **What else is there besides trying to sell more?**

> I have no specific list of questions to ask prospective clients for qualification purposes. **We don't really have a process to qualify prospects.**

> We have outdated presentations for everything under the sun. In most cases, I create my own.

> **Cold calling is dead.** If you do it, you will get stone-walled at the door. Of all the calls I've made, I can recall only once getting past the receptionist. People are comfortable with who they're using. At the end of the day, **all we're selling is a commodity.**

> We've not gotten testimonials or case studies from existing satisfied clients. I need to get them from decision makers, but **I'm not sure how to actually do it.**

> I like to go into companies, ask them what they are buying, and **figure out how I can beat them on price.** We're not the lowest price and it's hard to compete.

> We're all over the map in reps' ability. It's like there are a bunch of **mavericks in the field doing whatever the heck they want.**

> Most of the training we've had has been product training—**no best practices and little, if any, consultative sales training.** I use my skills from my last company. I've had to watch and learn.

Do any of these sound familiar to you? If I interviewed your team, would people say similar things? Or perhaps something even worse?

The good news is that if you *were* to hear this, you wouldn't be alone.

The *better* news is that each of these quotations represents an issue that can be fixed. If you're able to solve these problems, understand what's missing, add what needs to be added, and remove what's bogging you down, you have a massive upside—as long as you execute.

TAKE A MOMENT, STEP INTO THE FUTURE

Imagine it's twelve months from now. All the answers to the true-false questions are now true, and your team is no longer making those derogatory comments.

What impact would that have on your company's growth? What would it mean to your margins and profitability? On a personal level, what would it mean to your own career? To your income? To your family? To your happiness and personal fulfillment?

Know that the very first step to improving your results is to become fiercely honest with yourself. If you can do it on your own, then great. But, if you are the leader of the organization, you have to be wary of people simply telling you what they think you want to hear.

If you believe that may be the case, then you may consider having an independent group conduct your audit. For information on this go to www.salesedgetoolkit.com.

CHAPTER 4

BUILD YOUR CORE POWER MESSAGE

NAVIGATE OUT OF THE "SEA OF SAMENESS"

What is your company message and how well is that communicated by everyone in your company?

Who needs to fully understand that message and be involved in communicating it? Your whole team—sales, management, leadership, marketing, and customer service.

I'm not talking about writing an elevator pitch. While the thirty-second "who we are and what we do" statements were powerful in the 1990s, they are far less effective in today's buying environment. Decision makers are busier than ever before, which means the new playing field requires a different approach. To be effective, you must build messaging focused on the problems and goals of those decision makers and on what you can do to improve their lives and circumstances.

This—what makes you the unparalleled solution—is *the foundation* of your Core Power Message.

Your Core Power Message is a consistent and powerfully written communication that edifies who you are and how you help the people you serve solve their most pressing problems. It is centered around what they want and need from you. *Not* about you.

INTERVIEW WITH A BUYER

Top things that I do not care *about:*

- *Your company history*
- *Filling me with buzz words*
- *You asking me to listen to your stuff*
- *Meaningless information that does not pertain to me*
- *I don't care that you own XX percent of the market*

This is all about me. What can you do to help me get to where me and my company want to go? Anything outside of that is a waste of time.

—BRAD R., PRESIDENT/PARTNER, BUSINESS PROCESS OUTSOURCING

The Core Power Message becomes the core content for how you market, sell, and ultimately communicate.

Here's the challenge: most companies have no consistent messaging strategy. Those who do have one make it all about them: "this is who we are and why we're the best choice," "this is what we do," "this is who we help." Even in industry-leading companies, there is a tendency to rely fully on the marketing team to create and distribute the message. Participation or buy-in from the sales department is a rare commodity. And these are the people who speak with your target audience every day.

SEE YOUR DECK FOR WHAT IT IS: A STOP SIGN

To become the ultimate strategist requires you to build a consistent Core Power Message.

Here is a real-life example:

In talking with one of my client's salespersons, I asked, "When you meet a client for the first time, what do you do?"

He paused briefly and said, "Well, I try to deliver our corporate deck, but it's too long and it's terrible. Do you want me to send it to you?"

"No," I replied. "But, let me guess. It says who you are,

the history of your company, what you do, how you do it, your signature client logos, and so on."

He chuckled, "How did you know?"

I said, "How many slides is it?"

"Seventy-three…"

Ugh!

INTERVIEW WITH A BUYER

Ninety percent of people bring in a presentation with seventy slides. If you did this, I would flip past all the bullshit (when we were founded, our client logos, etc.) I will literally rip the presentation away. This is all about ME—what can you DO FOR ME? Tell me more about how what you said on the call relates to my problems. If you like, I'd be happy to go through how we do business. Very small percentages say "I'd love to hear about your business." Most initial meetings are worthless, but I have to do them to find that needle in a haystack partner.

—BRAD R., PRESIDENT/PARTNER, BUSINESS PROCESS OUTSOURCING

Most companies we work with are dealing with the same situation. Usually, their "message" is created by their marketing team and is built on the following:

- **About us**
  - Problem one: people don't really care.
- **All of your locations**
  - Problem two: people *really* don't care.
- **What we do (in all its detailed, technical glory)**
  - Problem three: this is where they start to fall asleep.
- **All the brands that you sell to**
  - Problem four: at this stage, you have totally lost them.
- **Your tag line**
  - Problem five: your audience is now checking emails and messages on their cell phones.

Now, keep in mind, if this is close to your "Corporate Deck," then know that you are indirectly teaching your sellers the *wrong* way to sell.

What every company needs is a Core Power Message; that leads to their Power Deck. A Core Power Message is *not* just about you. It is about *them*. Let's face it—unless it's your mother, people care far less *about you* and much more about *what you can do for them*.

FOUNDATIONS OF UNDERSTANDING

A Core Power Message has four primary parts, which I'll detail below. Before we dive into that, however, it's important to understand these four basic principles:

1. What makes you different?
2. What difference does your difference make?
3. What are the key problems you solve?
4. What could be your buyer's fears?

The principles exercise works much better when you involve the team in workshops. Call a meeting with your team members, including marketing and sales. Then, conduct workshops and discussions to brainstorm the four elements of your Core Power Message. Get the teams to buy into the process and provide their feedback as you refine the message.

Remember, when *you* say it, they may not get it. When *they* say it, *they own it*.

Understanding Competitive Parity vs. Your Competitive Advantage

This is called Competitive Parity. It goes like this:

Customer: "How is your quality?"

Seller: "Excellent."

Customer: "How about your service?"

Seller: "Amazing."

Customer: "Well, your price seems too high."

Seller: "Well, where does it need to be?"

Sound familiar? And companies wonder why discounting to win deals is happening so much!

Bottom line, you must stop competing with Competitive Parity.

Here is the problem: if you look like, sound like, act like, and sell like your competitors (Competitive Parity), then your only way to stand out (due to perceived commoditization) is going to be on price.

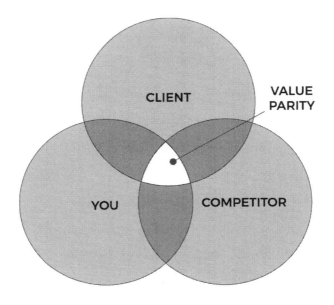

Rather, you need to focus on your Value Wedge.

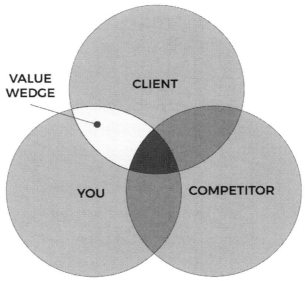

Three Value Conversations; Tim Reisterer, Erik Peterson, and Conrad Smith; https://corporatevisions.com/resources/books/the-three-value-conversations/

While the Value Wedge acknowledges where you are compared to others (Value Parity), more time is spent focusing on "what really makes you different." This is, without a doubt, where you need to spend the bulk of your messaging and selling time.

The Foundational Language Patterns of Key Decision Makers

Traditional sales taught us to sell value. Selling value meant that you adequately described the key principles of your offer in the form of price, quality, and service. It's a foundational technique inspired by the work of Tom Searcy and Barbara Weaver Smith in *Whale Hunting: How to Land Big Sales and Transform your Company*. This simple approach to improving your messaging can begin to take you from a "same-old" message to a message that truly communicates your prospect's concerns.

It's called, "The Sales Death Trap," and all decent-performing sellers know and use it.

If you communicate like your competitors, your only differentiating factor is going to be price. The Sales Death Trap puts you on the fast road to commoditization. It's the core of most companies' "discounting to win" strategy.

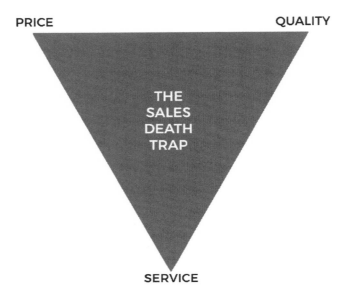

PRICE QUALITY

THE
SALES
DEATH
TRAP

SERVICE

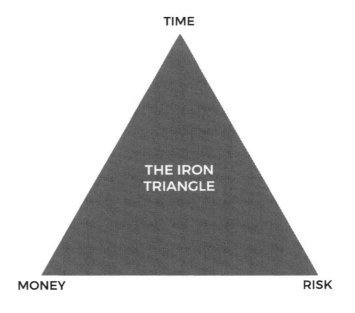

TIME

THE IRON
TRIANGLE

MONEY RISK

Focus on the "Iron Triangle" of Sales

Today, smart buyers are focused on three key areas. The faster you shape your language patterns to how they think, the better your overall communication will be with them.

Decision makers are focused on:

Money (vs. price). Smart people know that cheaper is rarely better. You must have confidence in having the money conversation, including leading assertive discussions on why you *are* more expensive. Your reasons may focus around total cost of ownership, your service or support process, better warranties, longer-lasting products, etc. One of the best ways to discover how to justify your pricing is to understand why your best clients currently buy from you. Once you identify that information, utilize that knowledge to benefit your potential clients. Those points *must* become part of your Core Power Message.

INTERVIEW WITH A BUYER

Cheaper is rarely better. If I make the cheap decision and it backfires on me, then my career is on the line. I must make smart money/budget decisions.

—SCOTT L., VP NORTH AMERICA, STRATEGIC SOURCING

Risk (vs. product quality). While both are important, know that decision makers are always thinking about making safer decisions. This includes reducing risk. How does your product, service, transition process, and/or your research process help your prospect know that choosing you is a "safer" decision? Are you super strong at explaining your warranty process or your guarantee process? You want to be proactive at explaining how you and your product/service are a safer decision—and how you can reduce any fears around the risk of choosing you and your company.

Time (vs. service). How does what you do help your client/prospect save time? How does it help their employees do more or perform better? Show them documented evidence to reinforce your claims to improve their capabilities. Make sure these results are being regularly communicated by both your selling and marketing teams. Look, every company is trying to do more with less. Spend time on your messaging to be able to elaborate on how what you do will help them be more productive in a faster way.

By simply adjusting what you say and how you say it, using the framework above, you will be head and shoulders above the normal communication that your prospective clients are receiving.

Now, let's get into the framework of building your Core Power Message.

PRINCIPLE-BUILDING WORKSHOPS

As previously mentioned, I recommend that you bring your key team members into a room and engage them in workshops to build the four principles. As you tee up the subject matter below, give your people two minutes to think about and write down their responses to the topic prompts. Then, facilitate the workshops.

Workshop 1: Clearly Defining "What Makes You Different."

> *Different is better than better.*
>
> —SALLY HOGSHEAD

Remember, it is likely that 90 percent of what you do is perceived by the marketplace as commoditized, or the same. Therefore, by today's standards, you have to be very clear on the reasons why your best clients continue to buy from you. These reasons make up the foundation of what makes you different.

Again, if you look like, act like, communicate like, and sell like everybody else, your only differentiation will be price. With every dollar you give away as you try to price match or discount, you're giving away a dollar of profit.

> Every dollar you give away is 100 percent profit.

Great companies focus on what makes them *different* from everyone else. What could make you different?

- The consultative approach that you offer
- That you're local
- Having a national presence (if it applies)
- The years of experience you and your team bring
- The attention to detail you provide

- The longer life cycle of the product that you have, compared to cheaper options
- Your unmatched customer service
- Your impressive response times
- The unique approach you bring to the market

In other words, there are always reasons that your best clients are buying from you right now and are gladly paying more for your products. Have you ever asked them, "What is it about us that stands out? What is it that causes you to choose us over our competitors?" When you ask those questions to your existing clients, you're going to hear the answers that will help you define, hear, and understand what truly makes you different. Write those points down. They are what you need to market effectively, and will be key elements of your Core Power Message.

Workshop 2: "What difference does your difference make?"

In the past, this may have been called the "benefit set" of what you do. This element is far more relevant to your audience because, whether they say this or not, it's the *most* important piece of the puzzle. However, unless asked, most sellers forget to discuss these details.

These workshop questions will help you establish your difference that makes the difference:

- Why do your unique differences matter to the buyer?
- How will their business change for the good?
- How will it help them simplify their life and reduce risk?
- How will it help them reduce their overall spend?
- How does it help them speed up time, create more efficiency for their employees, or take workload off their employees' shoulders?
- How does it simplify their buying process?

You've all heard the phrase "buying is emotional, then justified by logic." The difference that your difference makes is that emotional trigger. Remember, if you have a premium price, then you need a premium story.

Workshop 3: "What problems do you solve for your clients?"

> Your key to sales success is to attach yourself to a higher order business problem."
>
> —TOM SEARCY, *THE WHALE HUNTER*

One of the easiest and fastest ways to penetrate an untapped organization is to articulate your response to this question with precision and specificity.

> The "dirty little secret" about becoming a manager is, the higher you go, the more time you are spending solving problems.

These key questions will lead you to the answers you need:

- What are the problems and common frustrations your target audience faces?
- What are typical issues that others with their same title face?
- What are the common challenges that companies and people in your industry experience?
- What are some of the traditional inefficiencies that most companies struggle with?
- Which of these problems do you ultimately solve for your clients and how?

INTERVIEW WITH A BUYER

Get ME to talk. About my problems—general problems to distinct problems. Have me lay out everything that is wrong. Also, be prepared to talk about other problems that you are seeing and solving in the industry. Be prepared to share a case study or two with relevant companies to me.

—BRAD R., PRESIDENT/PARTNER, BUSINESS PROCESS OUTSOURCING

The reason people will choose to change is because there is a problem that is not being solved—or they are trying to accomplish something new and need external help. You have positioned yourself to solve it better than their current provider or their current process.

Workshop 4: "What are your buyer's fears?"

Hidden objections are deal killers. Have you ever had a big opportunity on the line where everything was looking good, you had submitted and presented your proposal, it seemed like you had a great shot at winning, but then—the deal just went dead? Radio silence from the buyer. Now what? You follow up and nobody calls you back. Your deal sits in the "proposal phase" of your reporting, and now the boss is calling, wondering what is going on.

This usually happens because there was something unanswered during your sales communications.

Buyers may be dealing with hidden fears:

- The transition process to a new vendor: you need to lay that out for them proactively
- The salesperson (or you) are being deceptive or dishonest: you need to edify your bio, and your company histories of success
- You will do what you say you will do: show them case studies of companies like them that have chosen you, and are glad they did

- Having that difficult break-up conversation with their current vendor: offer to help them with the communications
- The "fear of the unknown" after having used the same vendor for many years: this is where you proactively share your case studies and industry awards

In all these cases, you have to do two things: first, uncover the hidden fears and objections; and second, address each one by clearly showing them how the pain of staying the same is far greater than the perceived pain of making a change.

Here is the key: don't wait for them to ask these questions. Proactively share this information during your presentation.

You must clearly explain how the pain of staying the same is greater, otherwise they won't change. You have to uncover the business problems they're experiencing, identify what kind of strain those business problems are causing the company, and describe what it's going to mean to the company if they solve these issues by working with you. Or, better yet, what could happen if they don't.

Four Workshops for One Purpose

The four elements these workshops are designed to draw

from your team are essential to defining your company's Core Power Message. After you ask these questions, you must collect the information, organize it, and refine it into a consistent message that's usable, repeatable, and persuasive. Then, require everyone in your organization to memorize it.

This will become your Core Power Message.

BUILDING YOUR CORE POWER MESSAGE

Now that you've established the foundational elements, let's discuss the four key frameworks of your Core Power Message:

1. **Your Introduction Frame**
   A. Example: "With over (XX) years of expertise, (your company) has established itself as the leading (what you do) company, serving (geographic areas you serve)."
2. **Your Problems Solved Frame**
   A. Our clients turn to us when they are:
      i. Burdened by...
      ii. Frustrated with...
      iii. Tired of dealing with...
      iv. Looking to solve the problem of...
      v. Trying to...
      vi. Looking for options in dealing with...

B. Note: It is key that you *anticipate* the problems your target company/position title is likely dealing with.

3. **Solution Frame**
   A. We solve these problems by offering:
      i. Your difference #1
      ii. Your difference #2
      iii. Your difference #3

4. **Your Proof Frame**
   A. With more than (installations, sales, etc.) in the market, we are helping companies like (name two or three of your signature clients) to solve their issues and create results for their company and clients.

The following example incorporates the principles and the four key frameworks, building a successful Core Power Message. Use this example to help you identify ways to utilize the information you've learned in this chapter and build the Power Message that will make your own company's value stand out among its peers and in the eyes of potential clients.

Here is an actual Power Message developed for one of our signature clients:

Since 1983, ███ has been the premier provider of ███ in the workplace. Our focus on maintaining a local touch with our clients while dominating the global market ensures our business/other vertical customers have expert consultation when it's needed most—with the ███ to make sure they have what they need when they need it.

Our brand works as hard as you and your team do, consistently evolving and expanding our product line to ensure we support your ███ workforce whether they are in the office, on the road, or at 30,000 feet.

We work with companies just like you to make your business and workforce more flexible, productive, ███. Companies turn to ███ when they (pick one or two of the following points depending on your audience):

- Are tired of extensive ███ and want more reliable solutions for their workforce;
- Need to reduce the cost of ███ support related to unreliable or outdated ███;
- Want to address ███ issues due to downtime, support requests, or service needs with their ███;
- Are experiencing difficulties in supporting ███ in their ███ environments;
- Are experiencing increased ███ issues and costs from

implementing a ▮▮▮ environment that needs additional support or resources;

- Are transitioning their workforce to ▮▮▮ and need expert consultation on ways to reduce risk, save time, and create ROI;
- Have reduced ▮▮▮ and are transitioning to a ▮▮▮;
- Are overspending on brand-specific solutions that may not support ▮▮▮, new device options, or technology enhancements;

Our dedicated experts are focused on helping _____ (*industry*) _____ (*titles*) who are frustrated by the constant change in ▮▮▮ standards and unreliable products that have a higher overall total cost of ownership. We do this by (pick one or two of the following points depending on your audience):

- Consistently investing in our product offerings to ensure ▮▮▮ to meet your business' technology needs now **and** in the future;
- Offering a wide variety of products and solutions through a single provider that can ensure you have the best options for your business needs;
- Providing a consultative approach that helps business leaders address unforeseen issues and challenges;
- Proactively addressing issues, ▮▮▮ challenges, adoption concerns, or product/service concerns;
- Providing lower total cost of ownership through reduced

support, service calls, and labor staffing to support internal service requests;

- Researching, testing, and optimizing to ensure we can always provide your leadership with best practice advice on projects and products;
- Providing a comprehensive support team of █████ that can help to prevent issues before they happen and handle them quickly when they arise.

Companies who work with (your company) have seen incredible results including increased █████ productivity, improved total cost of ownership, reduced █████, and decreased █████ expenses.

We work with (companies) just like yours, including (named clients).

HOW YOUR POWER PLAYS IN

Now that you have created your Core Power Message, what do you do?

Require your team to memorize it!

Here is what happens when you and your team commit this valuable insight to memorization:

It will start to leak out in their future conversations.

One of the best ways to assure consistent and highly persuasive messaging is to drive memorization first. Don't just ask for it; demand it.

In the next chapter, I will show you exactly how to use the details of your Core Power Message to create more appointments, drive more meaningful conversations, and successfully win new business.

PART TWO

ESTABLISH YOUR TARGETS, EXECUTE THE HUNT

CHAPTER 5

NARROWING YOUR TARGET LIST

Most Sales Teams Operate on an "Inch Deep and a Mile Wide" basis.

—GENE MCNAUGHTON

If you are responsible for hunting new business, this could be the most important chapter you read;

When you take a deep look at your target list of "prospective clients" think about the calls you are making as you and your team are hunting new business. If you are like most salespeople you are staring at a list a mile long, chasing every lead that seems viable. If that's the case, you're stretching your time and spreading your focus too thin to have a real chance at getting traction that will lead to appointments and meetings. You're hunting down everyone and anyone because, for most of you, you have to hit your target calling metrics. I get it; I've been there.

Establishing a more finite list of focused new business targets is critically important to expanding your sales and income. It's always surprising how few companies put time and effort into building their ideal target list. As a consultant, I consistently ask to see the list of accounts a salesperson or team is targeting. I typically get one of three responses:

1. The list doesn't exist
2. There's a list, but no one really uses it
3. The list is rarely agreed upon with management

The net result is that management is leaving it up to the whims of the salespeople to determine which accounts to go after, **if** they are going after new business at all. That is yet another thing we usually fix in our consulting relationships. And something that deserves huge attention.

Remember you only have so much time to hunt. So, you must use that time in the wisest way.

WHERE COMPANIES STRUGGLE

Let's first discuss key reasons why companies are struggling to prospect and win new business.

While this chapter is going to show you exactly what needs to happen to open more doors and set quality meetings faster, you first need to be able to identify core patterns you may be stuck in that are limiting your growth.

PROBLEM 1: RELYING ON MILK RUNS

Your most precious asset is your time. You only have so many selling hours in a day, week, month, and year. Choosing *where* you're going to spend your time is as important as choosing *how* you're going to spend your time.

How you spend your time involves the tasks and activities you do all day long.

But *where* means which accounts you're focusing on and prioritizing.

One mistake I see salespeople make is spending too much time going on "milk runs." This means they are going from existing account to existing account, checking in, saying hi, shaking hands, bringing donuts, and doing feel-good meetings to keep existing customers happy. While it's good to make sure your current clients are happy, what ends up happening is many reps spend a large portion of time on these milk runs and then struggle to understand why they're not meeting their numbers or their territory isn't growing at expected levels. This is referred to as the milk run syndrome, and it screams mediocrity. It's very hard to grow fast when this syndrome runs rampant in your company. Keeping existing customers happy is important (and *much* easier), but it's not how you exceed your growth goals. It could be the main reason you are not growing at the pace you want to.

PROBLEM 2: THE INCH DEEP AND A MILE-WIDE SYNDROME

Let's say you've made it absolutely clear that prospecting/hunting new business is important for you and your company. Great leaders mandate it, and it's an important first step. Yet, while the strategy is right, the tactical execution usually isn't. The mistake made by most companies/sellers is that they aggressively go after a large list of prospective clients, versus a smaller list—as we discussed in the beginning of this chapter. They tend to make one to two communication attempts to the contacts on their large list, expecting results (ie: a callback, an email response, a registration for something), and when they don't get the response, they stop their attempts and move on to the next one.

Research and experience say it can take between eight to twelve attempts to simply get the attention of the people you are going after. Let me make sure this sticks in your mind: one to two attempts (and this is 90 percent or more of all salespeople) rarely gets the job done. Get the point? Good.

Here's the other point you need to commit to practice: focus your time and energy on a smaller, more preferred target list and go after these companies' key contacts a *minimum* of eight to twelve times.

There isn't anyone you can't get to when you're persistent.

PROBLEM 3: YOU HAVE NO STORY TO TELL

Once you *do* get the attention of your key contacts, you have to be ready. Keep in mind, you have a very short window in which to make an impression and successfully persuade them to want to have a conversation with you. The problem is that most companies do not provide the training their salespeople need, specifically on language patterns, short sentences, and creating a compelling reason for the target to want to talk with you. One of the most effective and persuasive ways to grab the attention of a target is having a story that will connect and pique their interest.

HERE IS HOW YOU MOVE THE NEEDLE

Depending on your territory and priority focus, know that spending more time going after ideal target accounts (usually mid-size, or large) is the fastest road to growth. Let's face the facts: it takes just as long to close a small account as it does a larger account. Think about it in terms of the effectiveness of a shotgun versus a rifle. With a shotgun, the impact is spread out to a wide area. With a rifle, the impact is focused on one specific point and the effectiveness is undeniable.

Choosing where you focus your time will determine your effectiveness and ability to grow. We have to remind ourselves that we only have so much time to proactively go after new business. A shotgun approach is not the answer. A rifle approach is. Put forth the needed effort to identify exactly which companies you're going to target, then go after them relentlessly.

NEVER MISTAKE ACTIVITY FOR PRODUCTIVITY

Most reps will drive to a certain part of their territory, then call on every company in that area. They'll make ten calls in one day, so it feels like they're being productive. These reps usually mistake activity for productivity. Then they get to the end of the quarter, and they realize they were able to bring some small customers on board, but the impact on their quarterly number was miniscule. What is a more productive use of your time—closing and onboarding ten small companies or one giant company that can make your entire year? Use the rifle approach to identify your key account targets, then laser focus on them.

THIS SEEMS EASY, WHY ISN'T EVERYONE DOING IT?

Large deals are what can change the game, so why are more than 90 percent of sales teams going after small ones? The answer is in the question: they're *big*. The larger the target, the more intimidating it can seem. Salespeople tend to make assumptions in these situations: bigger companies are already working with the best—they already have exceptional services, exceptional reps, and deals that can't be outdone. That's not always the case. You have to change your mindset.

With so many reps making these kinds of assumptions,

larger companies are likely not getting a sufficient selection of services to choose from—ones that truly meet their needs.

Here's another question: How will you ever win a large company deal if you never go after one? When you spend your time chasing small companies, that's all you're ever going to close. You're going down a bunny hole that never ends. It's time to turn that around—to claim your part of that 10 percent that hooks that big fish, the Whale Accounts.

> *"In any marketplace, there are always a smaller number of best buyers than there are all buyers; and the best buyers produce far bigger results."*
>
> —CHET HOLMES

The next obstacle is that most salespeople have not been trained properly in hunting and winning huge deals. The key is committing to obtaining the best tools, the best strategies, the best resources, the best mentors, and the best consultants to help you do it. Learning how to hunt and win major accounts will change the face of your organization.

Why does hunting big deals take specialized skills? Because there are greater challenges when chasing bigger opportunities. Big deals can take longer. There is usually a more complex selling cycle. There are more people involved (we will refer to this as the "Buyer's Table"). You have to do more consultative work to uncover problems. The stakes are higher. But once you learn major account hunting skills, you will feel confident in going after big fish.

HOW TO SELECT PROSPECTS

The first step in hunting major accounts is establishing a key accounts target list. This is different than the list you make when you're planning on blanket selling across a large area of targets. This list is meant to laser focus your time and energy on a smaller ideal target list—not make the target list you have even bigger.

Start by looking at your list of existing clients. Don't just list their names on a page. Create a spreadsheet that allows you to rank your existing customers by total revenue, total profit, current volume, potential volume, and any other metrics that are meaningful to your organization. In other words, establish your current Best Buyer list and organize them by rank.

THE PARETO PRINCIPLE AND WHAT IT MEANS TO YOU

Take a look at the spreadsheet you've made of your current clients. Now look at how many of those are your top buyers.

Chances are, a large portion of your revenue is heavily focused on a group that consists of about 20 percent of your client list. Think about the time and energy you've put into getting deals with all your clients. Now, think about how much revenue you'd have if you took that same time and energy and focused it on growing that 20 percent of your best-buyer companies. What would it mean to your revenue and to your company's overall margins if you doubled your number of best buyers?

Now that you know who your best buyers are, take note of their similarities. What sets them apart from the other 80 percent of your accounts? Put together clear criteria to help you identify their characteristics, making sure to include tangible and intangible characteristics. By doing this you will be able to make your shorter list of ideal clients to call on.

First are the tangible criteria—this usually includes company size, industry, geographic location, sales volume, revenue, and profit. Are they the size of your ideal clients? Does it make sense geographically for you to target them? Are they part of an industry or a vertical within which you already have a good story to tell because you have existing clients there?

Then the intangible criteria—include whether you can have access to senior level people, whether their company values match up to your company values, and whether you solve a problem for companies like this. You're also looking to see whether they're willing to make a change in suppliers, how long their sales cycle is, whether they have brand recognition, and what their political environment is like. This information will become available when you begin having conversations with them.

Intangible Criteria

The things you cannot measure.

These items may vary by company or be more subjective in nature. .

Examples:
Access to senior decision makers
Level of commitment to innovation or growth
Alignment with corporate goals and strategies
Political or cultural environment
Company goals and objectives
Management climate, turnover, or staffing
Willingness to change or try new strategies

Tangible Criteria

The things you can objectively measure.

These items may numeric or financial, but are always easy to measure.

Examples:
Growth or revenue performance
Credit ratings or financial stability
Number of employees or desks
Number of locations
Fleet count or asset count
Revenue per employee or location
Profitability or stock measurements

> Create a list of your best potential buyers and you will know *where* to best spend your prospecting time.

It's important to keep in mind that every potential client that meets certain tangible criteria will make it onto the first list. The intangible criteria, however, will help you narrow down that list. You may find that while a certain company is the right one to target, other criteria may reveal the company isn't one you want to do business with. For example, the company may be one that has top revenue and is your target market, but they're locked into a contract with their current supplier or hold values that conflict with your own company values. You're going need to have the discernment to disqualify potential clients and move them off your best buyer list. Great sellers are always better at disqualifying opportunities early in the cycle.

PRIORITIZE YOUR TARGET LIST

Next, you need to determine the best order in which to attack your list. Do this by ranking your criteria by order of importance. For example, if your company is located only in the Midwest and you don't have the ability to service clients outside of that region, geography will be ranked high. If you're in Florida, this may cause you to move a potential client based in Iowa to the bottom of the list or remove them altogether. Ranking and prioritizing based on the characteristics that are most important to your company will help you further narrow down the list. What you'll be left with is a highly-focused list of prime targets that you can use the rifle approach to go after.

Don't worry if your final list is only a handful of companies. The more clarity you have about what you're looking for, which companies you're targeting, and why they're your top prospects, the more likely you are to be successful hunting them. To put it another way, you will *not find* what you're *not looking for*.

Here is a great client example. I was working with an engineering client out of Nebraska that had three additional satellite offices in neighboring cities. As I was looking at their pipeline reports, I noticed a key target account, a very well-known company out of Beaverton, Oregon. After going through this exact content, I asked them to help me understand why they were in pursuit of a company that was thousands of miles away. The proud Sales Executive in charge said, "They are a huge brand, and we had a connection there. In fact, we are flying out (by saying "we" he meant himself and two others) on Friday for our first meeting with them."

I said, "So, let me get this straight. The three of you are flying for several hours, renting a car, and staying in a hotel on the other side of the country for a one hour meeting?"

"Umm yes," he said.

"And given the rare chance that you have a second, third, or even fourth meeting, that means even more travel, more rental cars, and more hotels?"

"Well, yes," he said, now with less enthusiasm.

"And if you win," I asked, "how do you plan to actually conduct your engineering services? Would that mean you would have to fly your engineers there, house them, and pay for their living expense?"

"Um, yea, I guess so."

I said, "How in the world would you even be cost competitive with that additional overhead?"

I looked over at the CEO, who was in the room. I felt the cold stare.

I said, "There are literally *hundreds* of ideal clients right in your back yard. Why aren't you spending your time hunting *them*?"

"Trip is cancelled," said the CEO.

While I wasn't popular in the moment, in terms of the business outcomes, I was right.

Spend your time in the areas that can produce the greatest results. Focus on high-impact areas, not low-impact areas. It takes just as long to call a two-million-dollar company and schedule an appointment as it does a hundred-million-dollar company and schedule an appointment.

By this point, you've looked at the companies on your list of prospective clients and you've narrowed down the list to key best buyer accounts that can move the needle. You are committed to taking the rifle approach instead of the shotgun approach. The next step is going after the accounts on that list.

You have to get proactive.

You must build and implement a formula, a strategy, and a methodology to go after these target companies and key contacts in a consistent and effective way.

Before you move to the next chapter, let's take a moment and understand what your BUYER is actually thinking about. Here is a transcript of an interview with a Senior Decision Maker:

Written by a professional buyer and decision maker:

I'm only as good as my suppliers/vendors/partners. I evaluate any company trying to become part of my supplier portfolio in several ways, from value to efficiency, to quality and reliability. The people are a big part of the equation. I must be picky because on-boarding a new supplier takes time and is risky. You're asking me to stake part of my career on you.

Who I Need You to Be

You need to be dependable, add value as a subject matter expert, provide great account coverage, and understand the industry and how to stay ahead. You need to understand my business and how you can help me grow, naturally growing alongside me. Be available when the "oh shits" happen, because they will. Be available to react to short lead times in order to gain unexpected business. Have a plan ready. Be a fan of the company you're trying to sell to, maybe buy some of their products.

So, how do I choose who gets a meeting? It does start with first impressions, as stated prior. I need a partner that I can rely on. So, don't start off with lies (no confidential info about my competition) or gimmicks; you're immediately dismissed. I look for these qualities:

1. Know your product/service
2. Know the industry
3. Know my business
4. Anticipate problems that I am working on
5. Know the history of our relationship

Integrate the above three into how your widget/service is going to save me time and/or money. How are you going to make my life easier? If you do these things, and your subject matter is something that is important to me, then we will have a meeting.

To start the meeting, be on time, come prepared with NDA signed, and don't lie or hide any facts. I need to trust you. Bring a product expert or a field sales engineer with you, as I might have some deep technical questions to ask.

Character is Critical

Social Media: I might look at LinkedIn and check you out, make sure everything is updated and professional.

Most importantly, if I like you, I will trust you more. If you can show me how you can help me solve one of the many problems I am responsible for, then you have a shot. If I am driving a new project, and you have subject matter that I am researching, then I want to talk to you. My life is about solving problems, driving the business forward, helping my team be more efficient, and beating my budget. If you can fit into that mold and help me, my team, and my company achieve our goals, then you have a shot.

If you use old shifty tactics to get to me (phone, email, or social) you are automatically out.

If you come in with a corporate deck that is all about you, unless you are my only option, you are out.

If you hammer me with closing techniques to push me faster than I want to go, you are out.

If you do not have the answer, tell me you will find it. If I find you dancing around my questions, you are out.

If you push things on me that I do not want or need, you are out.

If you come to a meeting and talk the whole time, you are out.

You need to know what makes you different, why it matters, and how you are better than your nearest competitors. I love case studies and industry research. I love it when a salesperson asks me how he/she can help me the most.

I am your buyer.

Pay attention, and you just might win my business.

—JOHN G., VP SUPPLY OF CHAIN AND OPERATIONS

In the next chapter, I am going to show you exactly how to effectively hunt and win your ideal target accounts.

CHAPTER 6

LAUNCHING YOUR ATTACK

You can't launch old weapons on a new playing field.

When you study the habits of top performing sales hunters, you realize that they have a multipronged attack. It's not just about making calls; it's also about how they email, how they show up at networking events, how they deliver sales presentations, and how they conduct themselves in the booth at a trade show. In most cases, they effectively use social media and have a stellar online presence.

If you want to hunt and win, you must be proactive. To be truly effective at hunting business, you have to move away from old sales tactics and utilize new techniques. You have to have an integrated sales and marketing strategy.

OUTDATED TECHNIQUES

The most common problem I see in prospecting is salespeople who operate under an old system from the '80s and '90s that says prospecting for new business is all about call, and call some more. This thinking can lead reps to believe that the *only* key to generating new business is to boost their calling activity. While that can be helpful, it doesn't completely cut the mustard.

Activity is less important than productivity.

Managers assume that if a salesperson has been in sales for a decade then they must be good at bringing in new business. That's a fallacy. Just because someone does something over and over again does not mean they're doing it right, or even that they're doing the right things. I know plenty of golfers who have been playing the game for years, but with the same wrong form and poor fundamentals. And they never seem to improve their game. In sales, as in golf, if you repeat bad habits, you cannot expect to get improved results.

Very few companies spend time creating a system that is designed from the ground up to get more leads, move them to warm contacts, and engage contacts in a way that ultimately leads to successful meetings and closed sales. I see these same mistakes time and again. When we work with companies, I ask salespeople and managers to rate their proactive business generating process on a scale of zero to ten. Zero means it does not exist. Ten means they're hitting it out of the park. To achieve a ten, the company would have to be highly effective at getting appointments, running great meetings, understanding the new client's needs, making killer presentations, and converting prospects into customers by closing large deals. I have yet to find a company that realistically ranks above a five.

Even the companies that are aggressively targeting new business and are really going after big game are spinning their wheels. While they *desire* this outcome, the process is usually not strategic, nor even organized. There's no big-picture strategy controlling the steps and managing the process, and the company is not skill building in this area.

This is a shame, because hunting and winning new accounts is one of the most important needs in all businesses. A top performing sales team must know how to network, get more meetings, get in front of key decision makers, and bring in new customers.

There are several methods we're going to identify in this chapter that you could and should be doing. Here's the beauty: very few companies actually do this stuff. This is a tremendous opportunity for you to stand out, because no company that I've seen has a fully synchronized, soup to nuts, proactive strategy in place.

Bottom line: if you want to be a great hunter of business, it must be a designed, well-laid-out, systematized, and measured process.

CALLING IS ALIVE AND WELL

There is a lot of noise in the online sales world that cold calling is dead. Many so-called sales and marketing experts say that social media and digital marketing have replaced the good old fashioned cold call and salespeople don't need to pick up the phone any more. They say that cold calling is "a massive waste of time." That's crap! Only weak salespeople buy into that idea. Calling, as **one** of your strategic weapons, is alive and well. In fact, that piece should be mandatory.

I'm actually glad that this misinformation is out there in the marketplace—that means there are fewer calls being made now than any time in the last thirty years. I love that. Why? Because companies and sales teams that follow the system laid out in this book will set themselves apart and stand out in their market. I can tell you unequivocally and with 100 percent certainty that proactive calling is not dead; it's more effective than ever. If you do it right, you'll reap the rewards.

Here's what you need to know: cold calling is not about volume. It's not about "smiling and dialing" to maximize the number of calls you make. It's about sticking to the rifle approach we discussed in the last chapter and targeting specific titles in your ideal accounts.

> *"Dig your well before you are thirsty."*
>
> —HARVEY MCKAY

Be proactive about your approach, because you never know when one of your target accounts will have a change in their business. Without consistent, planned calling, you'll never know when the current supplier makes a mistake, raises their prices, has supply chain problems, or fails to meet a commitment. You must be in contact with your key ideal prospects so when there is a window of opportunity, you know about it. Opportunities *do* open up, but most salespeople miss out on them simply because they are not "top of mind" in the buyer's world. They didn't work to establish relationships early enough. They weren't having meetings *before* the prospect was in the market to buy.

WHY SALESPEOPLE SAY COLD CALLING DOESN'T WORK

Here's a typical cold calling scenario. Bob is a sales rep for a large manufacturing supply company. He has a client in a certain part of town, and the last time he went to meet with that client, he drove around the area and made a few cold calls. He just knocked on doors in an industrial park and said, "I was in the area and thought I'd stop by and introduce myself." After three or four rejections, Bob gives up and calls it a day. He thinks to himself, "This crap just doesn't work. It's a waste of time." In a way he's correct; cold calling like that never works.

Let's analyze Bob's actions. What are the problems with his approach? He's randomly calling on companies that he knows nothing about and has no list of key target companies. He has no idea which accounts are worth going after because he hasn't done his research: he doesn't know the names of any of the key people at these companies and has no useful market data or relevant industry information to share with them. Bob's using the shotgun approach: his actions and activities are random and haphazard. He is completely unprepared, with no planned talking points and no strategy. It's no wonder so many average performers like Bob say, "Cold calling doesn't work."

The data and my experience suggest that it takes, on average, eight to twelve contacts before you get the attention of a point person at a prospect company. Unfortunately, most salespeople give up after just one or two attempts. They'll send an email here, make a call there, but rarely get past the gatekeeper or get a call back from their voicemail. So, they give up. They have no plan and no strategy for follow-ups. Soon, they begin to dread proactive activity. If you're the leader of the sales team, you need to change this attitude by changing the process.

INTERVIEW WITH A BUYER

Less than one out of ten calls or emails I get are effective.

Basically, they are usually just a generic sales pitch with no personalization. It would be helpful if they DID read my company's web page and my profile, then actually worked to make a suggestion.

—LARRY B., DIRECTOR OF TOOLS AND TECHNOLOGY

FOCUSED PROACTIVE ACTIVITY

The way your salespeople structure and manage their time is critical to success. Since most salespeople rarely enjoy proactive work like cold calling, it often gets relegated to the time management category of "I'll get to it when I have time." As we discussed, that means it likely doesn't happen. It gets pushed off the plate. The only way to make sure your team is spending time each week going after their key target prospects is to have cold calling scheduled on the calendar and make each person accountable for it.

The best appointment setters and new business developers schedule time every week for proactively seeking new business. They block out everything else, shut down their email, take no calls, respond to no text messages, and focus on their list of key prospects. They block out two or three hours each week, minimum, and put their undivided attention on new business.

This focused time allows them to get into a proactive mindset. They have their CRM open, so they can track their activities, get into a proactive mindset, and get themselves into a rhythm. They have their ideal customer target list up on their computer and just before making each call, they review the key information on the prospect and know who to ask for. Their calling script/talking points are prepared and sitting right in front of them, as well as their voicemail script, in case they have to leave a compelling message. They know the key to proactive activity is not to sell their product, but to focus their energy on selling the reasons for meeting with them. They have a strategy and a plan, and their prospecting is organized, effective, and amplifies confidence with each conversation.

In contrast, when sales reps try to squeeze in proactive activities between meetings or while driving to an appointment or while sitting in the airport, it comes off that way. It's disorganized and random and unfocused, and the prospect will be able to tell.

MAKE PROSPECTING MANDATORY

Scheduling two or three hours (minimum) each week for proactive prospecting is so essential, good sales team leaders do not just recommend their reps do it, they mandate it.

Being proactive is not something you can leave to chance. It's not something you can just hope happens. Being proactive and scheduling proactive time is an essential and unavoidable strategy for growth. It cannot be ignored. It cannot be postponed. If your salespeople are constantly calling new prospects, constantly in the market meeting people, emailing, and following up on new business, then your sales will grow. Their attitude should be that they are moving the ball forward on their key prospects every week.

Remember, this cold calling should have a scheduled time on your calendar of two to three hours, *minimum*—pre-planned, blocked-off prospecting time each week. Two hours of a forty-hour workweek is only 5 percent. This may not sound like much time, but it's actually revolutionary and nearly unheard of in a lot of companies.

Doing this alone will set you apart from the pack of average performers.

COMMIT TO YOUR TARGET CUSTOMER LIST

There isn't anyone you can't get to if you're committed. Unfortunately, after two attempts, 90 percent of salespeople give up. Then they tell the sales manager, "That company is not buying."

To hunt faster and further, you must commit to a hunting *system*.

STACKED PROACTIVE ACTIVITIES

The best strategy I know for reaching anybody, including the president of the company, the CEO, or the business owner, is a system called stacked proactive activities (SPA). In essence, SPA means utilizing multiple methods of contacting someone in a strategic sequence that increases the power of the entire process. Those multiple methods could include phone calls, voicemails, email, marketing campaigns, social media, conferences, and even trade shows. If you are truly committed and you follow the tactics detailed here, then your chances of getting in front of just about anybody are very high.

The tactic is to "stack" these activities, which means to

implement each of them one after the other, but slightly overlapping each other. It works like this: first, the prospect sees an email from you. The following week he gets a voicemail from you. Then you start following him or his company on Twitter and LinkedIn and start making comments on his LinkedIn page and retweeting his tweets. The next week, you email an interesting article to the prospect with some news about his industry. Then you attend a conference where you finally approach the prospect and introduce yourself. Chances are, he or she is going to recognize your name and have some familiarity with you. This is an example of using stacked proactive activities—and it's highly effective.

Stacked proactive activities are a well-planned, multi-faceted strategy to go after your best prospects. This can be used to connect with key decision makers, VPs, and senior level people within your target companies. Stacked proactive activities focused on key people within your ideal accounts is the principle of hunting success.

PROACTIVE CALLS AND THE CORE POWER MESSAGE

In Chapter 4, we discussed the Core Power Message and how important it is to your sales success. You should have completed that exercise by now. If you haven't, it's critically important to the next steps that you stop and go through the process before continuing to read the rest of this chapter. You'll need to have your Core Power Message written and ready to go. Remember, your power message is your primary source for creating effective talking points (also known as the Access Messages) designed to capture your prospect's attention.

The Core Power Message is designed to be customer-focused. It's built around what you can do *for* the customer. Ideally, your Core Power Message will resonate with your prospects and persuade them want to meet with you. If it explains how your product solves a problem that your prospect is having or has had in the past, they will be much more likely to meet with you.

Once you've identified your power message, it's time to ask yourself, "How can we use our Core Power Message as the fiber and foundational language pattern of every proactive activity?" How you use your power message will determine how you stand out in a crowded market. You need to be able to apply it in every avenue of your outreach:

- How you convey it in proactive calls and voicemails
- How you implement it in emails
- How you work it into the conversation when you meet somebody for the first time or you introduce yourself
- How you incorporate it as you create social media content

- How you apply it as you network at a professional event or conference

There is a remarkable difference between proactive calls that are based on a clearly written Core Power Message, and those that are not. Most salespeople just pick up the phone and make calls without giving much thought to what they're going to say.

Here's an example of a weak proactive call with no underlying power message.

Salesperson: "Hello, may I speak with Robert Smith?"

Gatekeeper: "Who's calling please?"

Salesperson: "This is Gene McNaughton calling from Acme Company."

Gatekeeper: "What's this regarding?"

Salesperson: "I sent an email a few days back. I want to make sure Mr. Smith received it."

Gatekeeper: "Mr. Smith is very busy right now. I'll pass along your message."

Salesperson: "Okay, great. Thanks for your time. Please let him know that I called."

Weak!

This salesperson has no authority and is offering nothing of value. So, they get blocked by the gatekeeper. This is what 90 percent of salespeople do. This is the same 90 percent who tell their sales managers that cold calling doesn't work.

THE WEAK OPENING GETS BLOCKED EVERY TIME

Salesperson: "Can you connect me to the person who is responsible for buying (your products)?"

This opener gets you transferred to procurement, a place that you do not want to start at. *Double weak!*

Salesperson: "Hi, this is (your name) with (your company), I am going to be in your area and would like to come by to see you and introduce myself and tell ya a little bit about what we do here at (your company name)."

This opener tells the gatekeeper that you want to come by and waste an hour of their time for information they could find on the internet in less than five minutes. *Triple weak!*

The same thing applies to voicemails—weak equals ineffective.

Salesperson: "Hi Bob. This is Gene calling from Acme Company. Listen, I am going to be in the neighborhood talking with one of my other clients. What if I stop by and introduce myself, talk a little bit about what we do, and see if we might be able to help you out. Please give me a call back. Thanks. I look forward to speaking to you soon."

You tell me, if you received that voicemail message, would you return the call? No way.

KEYS TO SUCCESSFUL CALLING

Always remember: the next call you make could change your life. To be highly effective in making proactive calls, there are a few key elements to keep in mind:

First is your mindset. One thing that all successful pro-active sellers have in common is that they have a specific outcome in mind for every action they take. They have an outcome in mind before they even pick up the phone. Your *sole* outcome of focus when calling is to schedule time to have a meaningful conversation. But, real success requires more. It requires *attention* and *intention*. The greats always see the results *before* they happen. They visualize them. Visualize the person you're calling, that they're glad they got your call, they happily welcome you, and help you to take the next step. This takes only seconds and has a tremendously positive impact on your mindset, your attitude, and your end results.

Second, pay attention to your *tonality*. Research shows that *tonality* has five times more impact than the actual words you say. In other words, *how* you say something is more important than *what* you say. For example, have you ever asked someone, "How's it going?" They responded by saying something like, "I'm fine," but their tone was so somber and negative that you didn't believe their words? Listeners tend to believe your tone of voice more than the actual words you say. When you make proactive calls, make a point of coming across as a person of authority. One way to do this is to be sure and end sentences in a down tone, rather than an up tone. When you think of "up tone," imagine that girl from the movie *American Pie* who always started a story with, "This one time, at band camp..."

Third, realize that timing is everything. Anyone you're trying to reach is going to be busy. They don't have time to take courtesy meetings with salespeople. You may use all the calling techniques in this section perfectly, but still not get the desired result. That doesn't mean the answer is no. It simply means it's not enough of a priority right now to pick up the phone and call you back. Or, it could mean that what you're saying is not compelling enough to grab their attention.

Know that there is a tremendous difference psychologically between a hard "no" and a "not right now." Think about a customer who just purchased new technology one month ago. If you are calling that person to sell them new technology, it doesn't matter how great your product is or how amazing your voicemail message is, because the timing is wrong. They just bought new technology; it's unlikely they are even thinking about it...right now.

Another reason timing is important is because there is no way to predict when the right time to call is. That's why you have to keep at it. Business situations change. Competitors miss deadlines. There may be a new boss or leader in charge. The home office may set a new strategic direction. Just know that any number of things could make now the right time to get your foot in the door. If you're only calling on them once or twice a year, what are the odds you're going to call at just the right time? Slim. And even if your timing is right, you haven't consistently worked to build a relationship in advance of their need. So, by today's standards, random "once in a while" contacting rarely works.

You should look at the phone calls that you make and the emails you send just like any marketing campaign. Your goal is to create a positive impression on the recipient. There is a tremendous difference between a lousy, uncertain voicemail randomly left twice a year, and a consistent stream of highly effective, well-thought-out, absolutely certain and confident voicemails and emails left consistently over time. If you create a positive impression on the buyer, when the timing is right, there's an excellent chance they'll call you.

Fifth, always make sure your proactive calling campaigns are well-planned and have a beginning and an end. In the next section of this chapter, I'm going to describe a very simple voicemail/calling process. You will heavily contact certain individuals over the course of four to five weeks using multiple methods. Each one is different, and each voicemail leads to the next one. If the timing is right, you clearly identify the problem you solve, you mention companies you work with that are similar to them, and you clearly identify the benefits that those companies are getting from your product, then you're going to have a much higher level of success getting the meeting. If you are not successful getting the meeting, you'll simply wait ninety days and repeat the whole six voicemail process.

Sixth, whenever possible, you should be calling on multiple people within the same company at the same time and following a similar contact process.

The reason for this is that you never know where your first access point into a company is going to be. Preferably, it is at the decision maker/senior influencer level. But it doesn't always happen that way. You also can't predict which executives are going to leave the company, get promoted, or transferred to a different division. So, it's always smart to build rapport with multiple people at the same time.

INTERVIEW WITH A BUYER

We had a situation where a customer of ours got bunted up to me, due to a referral from one of my employees. The lesson here was that the salesperson had built a relationship with one of my employees, whom I had known for 15 years and had placed a high level of trust.

The main lesson: Treat everyone like they are a decision maker, even if they are not.

—SCOTT L. VP NORTH AMERICA, STRATEGIC SOURCING

Finally, be respectful people's time. When you call or leave a voicemail, keep it short and be concise. Aim to keep voicemails under seventeen seconds. If your prospect hears or sees a voicemail from you that is longer than this on her phone, she probably won't listen to it at all and will delete it.

THE SIX-STEP VOICEMAIL PROCESS

In this section we're just focusing on the science of leaving effective voicemails. At this point, you have your best buyers and the key people within those companies identified. You've blocked off time on the calendar to make proactive calls, you've clearly laid out your Core Power Message, and you understand the psychology and the rules of leaving great voicemails.

Let's dive deeper into how to create effective voicemail campaigns.

What I'm about to show you is statistically proven to create excellent results, but you must follow the process *exactly*. You also have to be impeccable on your commitments and time slots: call when you say you are going to call. The goal is to reach out to between four and six decision makers/influencers in a predefined period.

Why does this work? Because it has a beginning, a middle, and an end. It focuses on problems you solve, for whom, results your current clients are achieving, and offers to share case studies of similar organizations. It takes advantage of timing, and it's designed to open the door to the opportunity to have a scheduled time for a more meaningful, agenda-driven call.

Regardless of where you are in the calling cycle or

sequence, every voicemail must include at least two of the following five elements:

- Mention that you work with other notable companies in their industry: "We have had great success working with other companies like you, such as..." You're going to be viewed by the company you keep, so drop a few names—the more prestigious the better. When you namedrop your existing clients, it's more likely to have a positive effect.

- When you mention that you work with other notable companies in the industry, try to match the titles of people you work with to the title of the person you're calling. If I am calling a VP of sales, I am going to say, "Bob, this is Gene McNaughton calling from GrowthSmart. We work with sales vice presidents who are focused on..." Or if I'm calling a CEO, "Bob, this is Gene McNaughton calling with GrowthSmart. We work with CEOs who are struggling with..."

- Clearly identify two to three problems or frustrations that you solve and for whom. For example, "We work with vice presidents of sales who are working to win new business in the tech sector." Or, "Hey, Bob. Gene McNaughton calling from GrowthSmart. We work with sales vice presidents who are under the gun to grow their business, struggling to get new brands, and most importantly, they are having a really difficult time getting appointments in big companies." In this example, I've just laid out three very specific problems we solve and for whom.

- Mention specific quantified benefits that your existing clients are enjoying: "We work with Company A, and since working with us, they've seen an 18 percent increase in their new appointments and a 25 percent increase in new revenue."
- Always end with a call to action. What exactly do you want them to do? "If you'd like to learn more, call me back. I am sending you an email right now with specific times that I'm going to be able to meet with you." Or, "I am going to send you my contact information, so we can arrange the best time to talk." Always give them a very specific call to action.
- Bonus: Overwhelmingly, when asking your buyers about voice mails, they all said this: "If I received a voicemail that said you were referred to me by someone I trust and respect, you almost always get a meeting. It may be a phone conversation or a live meeting, but if you know someone that I know, I am likely going to talk to you.

If you received a voicemail like the ones above, and one of those problems is something that is on your radar, there's a strong likelihood that, at a minimum, you're going to check out my website or look me up on LinkedIn. There's even a probability that you're going to respond to one of my requests for a meeting.

SIX CORE POWER MESSAGE VOICEMAILS

First Call

- Hi, my name is _____ from (your company). We work with companies like yours who are in your industry and help (their title) to solve three key problems:
- *Examples:*
  - *Lack of consistent reliability*
  - *Concern about lifecycle costs*
  - *Wanting more consultative advice on...*
- I will call you tomorrow at (exact time) to discuss how we may be able to help you.

Second Call

- Hi, this is _____ from (your company). We work with companies like yours who are in the _____ business and specifically help (their title). Companies we have helped have achieved results like:
- *Examples:*
  - *Lower cost of ownership, including reduced spend on...*
  - *Professional and consultative advice on how to...*
  - *An increase in...*
- I will call you tomorrow at (exact time) to discuss how we may be able to help you.

Third Call

- Hi, my name is _____ from (your company). We

work with companies like yours such as (client one and client two), and help (name the title) to solve three key problems: (list anticipated problems from your Core Power Message). Companies we have helped have achieved the following type of results:

- *Examples*:
  - *Lower lifecycle costs*
  - *Professional and consultative advice*
  - *Reduced spending*
- I know you are busy, but if these items are important to you, here's my number: (xxx) xxx-xxxx
- For your convenience, I will call you in two days at (exact time) to discuss how we may be able to help you.

Fourth Call

- Offer a free educational experience.
- Hello (Client first name), this is (your name) calling from (your company). I wanted to personally reach out to invite you to our upcoming Executive Briefing, titled "4 Most Anticipated Trends in (your industry)." This will be a webinar, so you can join from wherever it is most convenient. We've shown this to other (titles) like you and have had raving feedback. If you are looking to further understand the most relevant trends in the industry, I encourage you to register today and pass the invite on to your team.
- I will email you the details. Hope to see you there.

Fifth Call

- Hi, my name is (your name) from (your company). Many other (their title) are turning to us to help them solve three key problems, such as:
- Examples:
  - Too many service complaints
  - Lack of attention
  - Concerns that they may be getting over charged
- I know you're busy, but please call me at (xxx) xxx-xxxx. For your convenience, I will be sending you an email that shares an important case study. You can expect a call from me at (exact next time) to discuss the information in the email.

FINAL CALL OF THIS SEQUENCE

- Hi (prospect name), this is (your name) from (your company). I know that timing is always important. It seems that the timing for our two companies is not right at this time.
- I don't want to be a pest, so I will reach out to you in a few months to see if your business issues have changed. So, this will be my last call until then.
- In the meantime, if anything changes between now and then, you can reach me at:
  - Phone, email
  - Thank you, and have a great day

FIVE-STEP LIVE ANSWER TECHNIQUE

Now that you have your specific voicemail strategy all planned out, it's time to think about what you'll say if the person you're calling **actually picks up the phone and says hello.** You'd better be ready for that, too.

Here is a simple five-step outline. I recommend that you actually *write this out* so you are not caught off guard:

- The attention-grabbing statement
- The bridge question
- The information give
- The ask
- Confirm meeting by proposing an agenda

THE ATTENTION-GRABBING STATEMENT

When you make your call, it's likely you *are* interrupting their day. If the person you're calling picks up the phone, you need to acknowledge the interruption by saying something like:

> "Pardon the interruption, Bob, I know you're busy. This is (your name) calling from (your company). I'm wondering if I can get ten seconds of your time to ask you a brief question."

As always, tone of voice is extremely important during the initial attention-grabbing phase.

THE BRIDGE

This is where you make sure you're speaking to the right person, and if not try to get to the correct person:

> "I'm curious, are you the person at (company name) who is most focused on (the outcome that your company typically provides)?"

If yes, "OK, great." Move on to the next step.

If no, "I'm wondering if you can point me in the right direction?" Followed by, "Would you mind transferring me over?"

THE INFORMATION GIVE

With this step, remember your Core Power Message points. This is where you mention a specific fact that might pique their interest or curiosity:

> "For over XX years we've been helping companies like yours to... (lower their spending, reduce lifecycle costs, protect the environment from contamination, etc.). Are you familiar with us?"

Think about and make sure you're pulling in the key areas of your power message here.

THE MEETING REQUEST

This is where you get them to agree that they are interested in what you just mentioned, and then ask them for a meeting:

> "Most (their title) are looking for ways to increase revenues while lowering costs regarding (your products/ services). Are those things important to you?"

> If yes, "When would be a good time for us to schedule fifteen minutes? I will share with you exactly how we handle that for (name a case study of a local/ regional client)?"

If they say yes to a meeting, "Great. Let's get our calendars out and get some time scheduled. How does this Friday look? 2:00?"

ALWAYS PROPOSE AN AGENDA

You want the meetings to stick, don't you? You have to give them a compelling reason to *keep* this meeting. This is your moment to put them at ease, tell them you're not going to try to sell them anything, and start taking control of the framework of the meeting:

> "I won't be giving you a bunch of sales speak, or show you a long, boring presentation. I'm guessing you will appreciate that (pause, use humor here).

> "I will get right to the point and be respectful of your time. If we can help you, then we will discuss any next steps at that time. But before we do that, I will show you samples of the companies we work with (or "I will share the details" if you are using your case studies), and how we help them specifically. In just fifteen minutes, you will know if we can help you.

> "I will send you an agenda in advance, and, at the fifteen-minute mark, I will stop. Then, you can decide if you want me to continue. Fair enough? Okay, what is the best email address?"

The last part is important because it helps ensure that the prospect doesn't get second thoughts about committing to a long, boring meeting. You have to give them a reason *not* to cancel.

ADDITIONAL PROACTIVE CALLING TIPS

- Always be clear on what you will do, and what you won't do:
  - "I won't waste your time with a bunch of sales speak or product demos. I will share with you what other companies like yours are doing to solve (priority problems/issues). If you see a fit, we can continue our conversation."
- Always discuss the value you will add:
  - "At the very least, you will find out how other (their title) are tackling key issues including (issue one, issue two, and issue three) and you will understand industry best practices as they relate to these issues."
- Always offer insights in the form of an executive briefing:
  - "We have researched (their industry) and understand many companies like yours are challenged with (issue one, issue two, and issue three). Many of these issues are being overlooked, and we are sharing our findings with a select group of executives. We'd like to come by and share these findings

in an executive briefing for you and your key team members."

EMAIL STACKING COMBINED WITH CALLING

During your calling campaign, you also need to commit to sending emails to your prospects. While just calling using the outline I gave you will be effective, you will supercharge your effectiveness by adding email touches to your outreach. But know this, *just* calling or *just* emailing alone is nowhere near the effectiveness of combining the two.

THE #1 KEY TO USING EMAIL

Your subject line will determine their action.

This piece *alone* will determine whether someone is going to read your email or not. Think about how you read emails on your phone. You are simply looking at who the email is from and the headline involved—and based on that alone, you will swipe left (delete), click it (open it), or do nothing intending to get to it later. That's why the headline means everything.

Here are some of my favorite email subject lines.

- "Just left you a voicemail." This can get people to read your email and listen to your voicemail.

- Another good one could be, "Three ways to reduce money, risk, and time." Remember the Iron Triangle of how leaders think!
- Another good headline is, "How we helped (company name or company description, if you cannot use their name) increase productivity 15 percent."

A different strategy is to announce the impact of a new trend, rule change, market disruption, or industry problems. Anything that's going to be pertinent to them has got to be in that email subject line. Stay away from long headlines; keep it concise. A good headline would be: "Three Keys to Navigating (the changing rules): What you Need to Know."

We had a client from Iowa who was in the debt collection business. There had been some new rule changes around the CFPB (Consumer Fraud Protection Bureau) that many large companies were scrambling to figure out. We immediately conducted market research to better understand the important changes and what it meant to their ideal buyers (large companies that outsourced collections). We built a fantastic educational briefing, along with a webinar. Every salesperson was given very specific scripts to invite both their existing clients, as well as targeted ideal prospective clients. They were also trained on a disciplined follow-up program for those who signed up and those who attended. Low and behold, one of the behemoth prospect company directors signed up. After following up (the right way), our client landed the biggest deal in that company's history—$125 million. Before this, they were a $60 million company.

Using the right strategy, offering education-based marketing, combined with a well-designed sales hunting plan, this company completely altered the course of its future.

EMAIL BODY COPY

When you get to the body copy of the email, follow these rules:

- **Always use the person's first name.** Any email that starts, "Dear Mr. Smith…" is usually seen as marketing spam and ignored. Start with, "Dear Bob," or even, "Hey Bob."
- **Then, go right to either the subject matter of the email or your headline**. "We have been studying the trends in the marketplace, and I'd like to talk to you about how you're handling these trends. I just left you a voicemail but would like to have a brief meeting to share with you how other companies are handling this."
- **As it relates to body copy, keep it short, and always have a call to action.**

BONUS MATERIAL

What *else* can you do to produce action from your targets?

As mentioned in earlier chapters, know that companies are, on average, 50 to 60 percent of the way down their research path before they will talk with you. My question for you is this: Where do *you* and your *company* show up along that timeline?

You have to *constantly* offer *valuable insight* into the market. Remember that market data is way more compelling than product data. Today, this is not the sole role of marketing. Successful companies know that research is the job of both marketing and sales.

Where to find compelling market data:

1. **Within your own company.** Many times, while working with a company, I discover that the marketing team *already* has market data. This could be trending reports, market expectations, competitive analysis, white papers, infographics, and even documented case studies. But it is *rare* that I find salespeople actually using this valuable information.
2. **Online.** Using Google, Twitter, LinkedIn, and industry trade websites, there is no shortage of trending information and market data. Know that *you* don't have to write it, you can simply repurpose information that has already been created. And guess what? Your buying team members are looking for this information.

How to use this material to gain access:

-   Use any and all market data as part of your email campaigns.
-   Offer to "share some recent insights" on your voicemail campaigns.
-   Offer a "Lunch and Learn" to discuss recent trends and breakthroughs in your industry.
-   Invite clients and prospects to join a webinar on industry changes, challenges, trends, or breakthroughs.

How do you combine all of this?

Let me show you a sample targeted campaign flow:

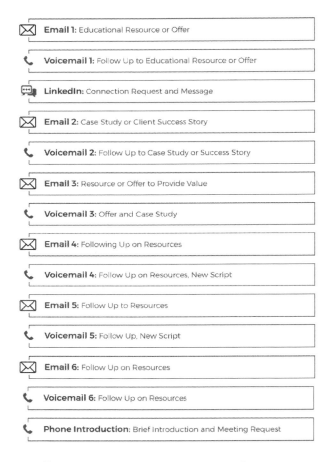

Email 1: Educational Resource or Offer

Voicemail 1: Follow Up to Educational Resource or Offer

LinkedIn: Connection Request and Message

Email 2: Case Study or Client Success Story

Voicemail 2: Follow Up to Case Study or Success Story

Email 3: Resource or Offer to Provide Value

Voicemail 3: Offer and Case Study

Email 4: Following Up on Resources

Voicemail 4: Follow Up on Resources, New Script

Email 5: Follow Up to Resources

Voicemail 5: Follow Up, New Script

Email 6: Follow Up on Resources

Voicemail 6: Follow Up on Resources

Phone Introduction: Brief Introduction and Meeting Request

Bottom line: you can get to *anyone*—as long as you are persistent and creative.

Friends, these *are* the best methodologies to get to anyone. When you use all or a significant number of creative techniques designed to offer value and target predictable patterns being experienced by a person's title, your meeting scheduling ratios will go through the roof.

But, this doesn't guarantee you are going to win more business. In order to win more business, you have to be prepared to run *stellar* sales meetings. So, keep reading, because the next chapter is going to show you how.

PART THREE

RUNNING THE ULTIMATE MEETING

CHAPTER 7

HOW TO RUN THE ULTIMATE MEETING

Good Salespeople have great answers. Geniuses have great questions.

It was the worst sales meeting I'd ever run.

Sometimes we learn our best lessons from our failures. The meeting happened during one of the lowest points in my career, but I credit it with completely turning my sales career around and putting me on the path to learning the secrets of being a top performer. I became determined to educate myself on the best way to sell.

It was one of the biggest companies in my territory. I was a corporate account executive for Gateway Computers but with very little corporate sales training. The target was a huge insurance company and my sales manager had put me in charge of getting in the door and winning their business. With no systems, no process, and no knowledge of the techniques I know today, I was operating on instinct alone—and my instincts told me to just pick up the phone and start calling every week until I got a meeting. So, that's what I did.

I called one of the senior executives at this insurance company week after week but never got past the gatekeeper. I was stuck, leaving unanswered voicemails and messages with his assistant. After three uneventful months, his assistant called me back and said, "John has agreed to meet with you. Can you be here Friday at 10?" I literally jumped with joy. I desperately needed something to happen, and this just might be my big break. I was struggling. My performance was low, my numbers were dismal, and my boss was putting pressure on me—my job was on the line. Hanging up from that call, I immediately called my manager and said: "I got a big one on the hook, and I'm going to land the account."

When I walked into the prospect's office that Friday, it quickly became obvious he was a top-level executive—the office was huge with wall-to-wall windows, couches, and a large desk. I was nervous. And intimidated.

"Young man I have to give you credit," he began. "You get

an A for persistence, and that's why you got this meeting. What can I do for you?"

I thanked him for taking the meeting and said, "I would like to ask you a few questions."

"No problem," he responded.

"How big is your company?"

He told me.

"How many employees do you have?"

He told me.

Next, I asked, "How many locations and branches are there?"

We were only five minutes into the meeting when he interrupted me. "Young man, I'm going to end this meeting right here," he said, "and I'm going to tell you why. I want you to remember this for the rest of your life."

My heart was pounding. Did I say something wrong? Did I insult him?

He said, "This meeting is over. And here is your lesson.

Don't ever get to a person of my level and ask basic questions about information you should already know. I have twenty meetings a day, and very seldom do I meet with salespeople. And this right here is the reason why: you just wasted my time. You should have already had all of that information. We should only be talking about what my problems are and how best to solve them. Or, if you know of a problem that I should be thinking about but I'm not. That's why you're here. Not to ask me obvious questions you should already know. Thank you for your time. Good day." And with that, he turned back to his computer and started typing.

I sat there for a moment in stunned silence. I was trying to think of something to say—some way to recover. A sequence of horrible thoughts and images flashed across my mind. What was I going to tell my boss? What would my peers say when they learned what happened? When I turned toward the door it seemed like it moved a hundred yards away. I had just blown the biggest meeting of my life. Three months of hard work down the drain. The walk of shame back to my car seemed to take an hour.

I realized that day that I needed to figure this out or find another career. I was doing something wrong. It had nothing to do with my product, my pricing, or the economy. It was all on me, and I needed to figure out a solution.

While the experience was humiliating, and I may have lost the fight that day, I will *never* forget the lessons I learned from that one painful meeting. After twenty-three years, I'm still telling this story, and still using it as a teaching tool.

WHAT I SHOULD HAVE DONE

Looking back, there are a number of steps I should have taken. I should have done a ton of research in advance, which would have put me in a position to walk into that meeting already knowing the answers to basic questions, like who their current supplier was and how they use their technology. I should have done industry research and known what areas they were likely to be having problems. I should have brought current market and industry data to share with him. I should have been able to tell him about some of the new best practices in the industry. I should have had a case study from one of our other big insurance company clients, or even big local clients. I needed to provide value, to be so well-prepared that I didn't waste a minute of his time.

But it wasn't total failure. Why?

That executive gave me one of the greatest gifts ever and triggered an immeasurably valuable turning point in my career.

You can lose the deal, but don't lose the lessons you learned.

Do you ever wonder why most companies rate "hunting new business" as the number one desired skillset, yet it's the *lowest* skillset among their sales teams?

It doesn't have to do with the market. It doesn't have to do with the buyers or whether you have the best product. It doesn't have to do with your price or the competition.

What makes the difference? Those first moments. It has everything to do with how your initial meetings happen.

If your salespeople are starting off by talking about your product quality, service, speeds, and feeds, they're quickly going to be relegated to the department that deals with identifying product specs and getting them at the lowest possible price. Procurement's job is to match you up by specs with your two or three competitors, and say, "You all do the same thing. Whoever can get the lowest price wins the deal." They *want* you to feel commoditized.

You've now been resigned to a price-sensitive selling cycle where your margins get squeezed. And this is *not* a profitable way to run your business.

> Great sellers *do not* lead with features and benefits. They lead *to* features and benefits.

Most salespeople have a natural tendency to start their meetings by immediately talking about themselves, their company, and their products, before learning anything about the customer. The focus is so much about their own goals that they don't spend time having meaningful conversations with the buyer to find out what their needs are and how they can best meet them.

That's exactly the path I took in the beginning. And it didn't work.

And then it all changed.

Listen to me—learn about my problems. I only care about what you can do for me. Get me talking. Earn another meeting. Be different. Have me write out my business plan on a white board. Do something different than pushing your agenda on me.

Find out who else should you be talking to

- *Technical person*
- *Financial person*
- *Can you talk to people who will be involved?*
  - *Can you call them directly?*
  - *Would you call them, or help set up a meeting?*

Just don't come in and give me a big presentation without knowing what my business issues are.

—BRAD R., PRESIDENT/PARTNER, BUSINESS PROCESS OUTSOURCING

ENTER SPIN SELLING

When my struggling career in field sales came to the point of "figure it out or get out," I called the top performer in our division and asked for advice. I wanted to know what he was doing that I needed to be doing. He said, "Do yourself a favor and go buy the book called *SPIN Selling*. *But...* don't just *buy* it, *use* it. You seem to be able to get meetings, but it appears that you're not running the meetings as good as you should be. This book will teach you how."

I went straight out and bought Neil Rackham's book—and quickly learned that the way I was selling was just plain wrong. I had been taught to get in front of a prospect, make a little small talk, show my corporate deck, do a product capabilities presentation, share spec sheets, and offer to put together a proposal. But that method wasn't working for me. After my presentations, I'd usually never hear from the prospect again.

As soon as I started implementing SPIN, everything changed. Reading and *using* the SPIN method was a landslide breakthrough for me. It was the first time I saw an initial meeting methodology laid out in a logical sequence, with questions that made sense.

SPIN Selling teaches the science behind asking the right questions, in the right order. There are four chunks of questions, each represented by one of the letters: S-P-I-N:

- **The S stands for *situational questions*.** Take time to understand your prospect's current situation.
- **The P stands for *problems*.** What are the problems the customer is experiencing? In this step, Rackham instructs salespeople to "find the pain and use it to your advantage."

- **The I stands for *implication*.** What is it going to mean if the client can't find a solution to this problem? What would it mean if the client solved the issue(s)?
- **The N stands for *needs payoff*.** In other words, if the seller can solve this problem would the buyer be willing to sign a deal? Or, "If we were able to solve this issue, what could that mean for you?"

Rackham's book was first published in the 1990s, but more than twenty years later, it's still a highly regarded book and a "must have" for your sales library.

I read the book and started to apply the techniques. As I continued to sharpen my SPIN skills, my dedication led me to land one of the largest deals in the history of Gateway Computers, which I talked about in the Introduction. Years later, I'm still teaching people the importance of asking the right questions in the right order.

The key takeaway is this: facing a rough road in your sales career doesn't mean you don't have what it takes. Find the right expert, study the expert's techniques, and work hard to implement their proven methodologies. You don't have to try to re-invent the wheel. Find the best people you can who are willing to help you. If you're leading a team, this is the key that will lead you to building a top-performing sales organization.

GIVING SPIN AN UPGRADE

As I got better at using SPIN, I began to win more new business than ever before. I was already good at getting meetings, but now I went in with a specific game plan and a high level of confidence. We had competitive products, competitive service, and our pricing was in line with our competition. What caused me to take business from my competitors was my ability to build great rapport, ask great questions, and build solutions to solve the issues, challenges, and problems that the clients told me they had. None of my competitors were doing that. I stood out in the market, not because of superior product or pricing, but because of the merit of executing a consultative approach.

But I began noticing a problem.

SPIN worked great in the situations where it made sense: when the customer was actually experiencing a known problem. That's where SPIN shines. But what happens if/ when the customer doesn't believe they have a problem? With no clear problem to solve, SPIN didn't work as well for me. My only option at the time was to offer to "stop by again in ninety days to see if business needs changed."

When I was selling computers for Gateway, every company already had computers. I found myself probing buyers with SPIN questions like, "What issues are you having in IT? What computer problems are you dealing with?"

In many cases, they'd say, "No problems. We're in pretty good shape. Everyone who needs a computer has one. They seem to work fine." Without a clearly recognizable problem, I had nowhere to go, nowhere to take the conversation, and no way to incentivize them to consider a change. Plus, SPIN recommended the use of questions like, "If I do A, will you do B?" and, "What would it mean for you to have that solved?"

After using SPIN for several years, I began to notice buyers become less interested by those types of questions. They were losing trust in me, sensing I was trying to sell them something. I could see *their* disappointment. I felt like I was going from being a consultative advisor to a crafty salesman every time I asked those types of questions (techniques from the past referred to as trial closes, double binds, and yes set questions).

That frustrated me. After working so hard to get the meeting—calling, writing letters (people weren't using email very much back then), stacking proactive activities, and finally getting in front of buying team members through persistence—I started to see promising opportunities slip away. More and more meetings were hitting roadblocks. Not only were they going nowhere, but even with the heightened techniques I had nowhere else to take them.

THE BREAKTHROUGH MOMENT

That's when I had an epiphany. I realized that my job as a salesperson was not *just* about solving perceived problems, it was about offering buyers a way to improve their situation. I needed to show them there was a reason to at least entertain the notion of change. I thought, "Maybe they don't think they have a problem, but what if I could provide them with a new way of looking at their business that could reduce their overall costs, improve efficiency, decrease downtime, or increase reliability in a way that would encourage them to want to hear more? With SPIN, if the customer didn't have a known problem, I was dead in the water. But under *this* scenario, the customer didn't need to have a "known" problem, per se, for me to go deeper in the initial phase of the process.

I realized that I had to find a *gap*—the point between where they are and where they want to be. If there wasn't a known problem, I had to find a way to show them how I may be able to make a current situation even better. If I could do this, I'd have a better shot at moving to the next phase of the selling/buying process.

My job became about establishing a gap between where the customer was at that moment and where they could be in the future. It still required me to fully understand their current circumstances, but more importantly, it drove me to further understand their company, division, and their departmental goals. Over time, I realized I needed to understand my key contact's *professional* goals as well. My job became about helping people move faster from their current state into their ultimate desired state. Everyone has a *gap*. There's always another level.

By shifting the questioning technique from identifying problems to identifying gaps, I was able to carry stronger conversations in just about every circumstance, whether or not the customer was experiencing an ongoing problem. If there wasn't a problem, I would ask simple questions like, *"If you could make your situation even better than it is right now, what would that look like?"*

That caused a deeper dialogue and helped me understand their full situation, their bigger goals, and, more importantly, find the gap. I soon realized, *if there is no gap, there is no sale.*

When you find a gap, you can open the customer's mind to new possibilities and new ways for making the existing situation even better.

This is where your experience with other companies and knowing your case studies can be a game changer.

OUT WITH SPIN, IN WITH THE EDGE

Through ongoing use of SPIN selling, but now enhanced by my experience and extension into a new way of client engagement, I created an altered questioning approach called The EDGE.

INTERVIEW WITH A BUYER

If someone is pushy or overbearing, they will not move to another meeting. Even if I HAVE to work with you, I will work hard to replace you.

—JOHN G., VP SUPPLY CHAIN MANAGEMENT

Similar to SPIN, EDGE is also an acronym. It's a road map to the four key question sets, the four pieces in the sequence that must be executed in a specific order. If you mix up the sequence—or skip over even one—you're going to reduce your chances of moving forward to the next meeting or next step in the process.

THE EDGE PROCESS – AN OVERVIEW

E = *Educate* yourself about the prospect, the company, the industry.

- How can I prove that I understand their business? What can I learn that will help me know them better and understand if I can improve their process?

D = *Develop* a gap between where they actually are now, versus their desired outcomes.

- What experience are they currently having, and what improvements do they envision for the future?

G = *Greater Gap* should be identified, so your target can see the problem you see.

- What will this mean in the future to be solved or not solved?

E = *Emotional* connection. This comes from "story," not features and benefits.

- What story can you draw from to connect effectively with your audience (i.e.: case studies)?

The first step in The EDGE process is crucial: *building massive rapport*. Rapport is the foundation of trust and is an important piece of educating yourself about your prospective company. Before you have a chance at holding an open discussion about a company's needs, your customers first must trust you. While most sales reps rely on their natural charm and personality, when you're hunting big deals you need a repeatable, reliable process:

Tool #1. Before the meeting, research the person you're about to meet. Doing your research ahead of time allows you to avoid awkwardly talking about traffic or the weather (weak conversation is reserved for weak sellers!). When you're relegated to making trivial small talk, you're missing a great opportunity to build meaningful rapport.

Today, looking up your prospect is easier than ever. Start with LinkedIn. Then do a Google search. Then look at their Twitter feed and other social media. Look for news updates, recent promotions, above all, look for things that you may have in common.

Ideally, you want to know two or three key facts about the person. For example, when you know where your prospect went to school, what they studied, his/her career progression, other companies they have worked for, and/

or even charities they support, then you have plenty of information to build meaningful rapport.

Tool #2. Do the needed research on the company and industry. Learn as much as you can about the latest news coming out of their company. Get on the company's website and find recent press releases. These give news about new products, financial results, mergers and acquisitions, awards they've won, expansions, new facilities, and executive hires and promotions. The press and media page of a company's website holds a wealth of useful information that can be used to build rapport and show that you've done your due diligence.

Imagine the rapport you will build if you open a meeting with, "I see that your packaging operation just got ISO9000 certified. Congrats. You oversee that division, right?"

Tool #3. Find reasons to give a sincere compliment without being obvious or sucking up. A sincere compliment can be as simple as, "So you're a vice president here; that's a big job." A sincere compliment demonstrates that you've done your research. It also communicates respect and professionalism. Surprisingly, doing this simple thing will help you stand out from most salespeople that your prospect sees.

Here is an example: I recently opened a meeting with a

senior executive team by complimenting their company's live stream of the Coachella Music Festival in Southern California the previous weekend. In some cases, people in the room didn't even know that the festival had happened. In just a few minutes of searching online, I knew the details and specifics outlined in the article I'd read, which opened the door to a great conversation about music and technology. Within the first ten minutes, I'd built a meaningful and genuine rapport.

INTERVIEW WITH A BUYER

Between all the vendors I have to choose from, I am always asking myself, "Who do I trust the most?"

—JOHN G., VP SUPPLY CHAIN MANAGEMENT

By researching the company before the meeting and taking just a few minutes to read through their CEO's Twitter feed, I had the latest news from the C-suite, learned about the company's new Sports Center in Las Vegas, their stock price, and, of course, the viewership of the Coachella livestream. Bringing these pieces into the first ten minutes of meeting conversation instantly established me as someone who was aligned with their company goals and their latest accomplishments. I earned likeability, trust, and respect. Having a strategy to build rapport is hugely important to the next steps of the process.

> **"When people like and respect you, they start to trust you. When they trust you, they will give you answers to the valuable questions you are about to ask."**

Now, let's talk about how to run a GREAT first meeting.

E = EDUCATE YOURSELF

After building rapport, it is time to start The EDGE process and educate yourself.

This is a fairly simple process. The easiest way to remember what you need to learn is with another mnemonic device: "The 5 W's and the 3 H's":

- *Who* is their current supplier/vendor?
- *What* is that supplier/vendor/service partner doing for them?
- *When* did you start working with them?
- *Where* do they provide their services?
- *Why* did you choose that supplier/vendor/service partner?
- *How* (#1) long have you been working with them?
- *How* (#2) are they doing for you?
- *How* (#3) do you measure whether that supplier is doing a good or bad job?

The more of these questions you can answer, the more

clearly you will see if and where opportunities may be present.

> Don't make this common mistake:
>
> Most sellers, if they've gotten this far, cannot wait to say, "Well, let me show you what we do," then go straight into their brochures, spec sheets, features, and benefits.
>
> Don't do this; it almost never works.

Be patient and move to the next step:

D = DEVELOP THE GAP

This is one of the most powerful elements of The EDGE process. If you don't understand and execute the D, it's unlikely that the prospect is going to consider a change and decide if there will be any next steps.

> REMEMBER: If there's no gap, there is no sale.

There are two keys in developing a GAP.

Key #1. Explore and discuss any existing problems the customer knows they're experiencing. Many leaders deal with a fairly high level of issues and challenges in their day-to-day operations, simply because that is what the nature of their role is. Every business has problems, right? Your job is to uncover and clearly identify these issues.

Ask some of the following questions:

- What kind of issues are you having now?
- What frustrates you most about the current situation?
- What happens when a ball gets dropped?
- What are your biggest headaches right now?

Key #2. Look for gaps between how things are right now and what "even better" could look like with a mind of exploration. Many people rarely think in these terms. They assume that if the assembly line is running without any major breakdowns or stoppages, then all is well in the world. But often, they're not thinking about how much better and more efficiently the line could run if they considered a few things. That's your job—to leverage existing client best practices and share how other companies are performing at superior levels.

How can you show them an even better way? Use some of the following suggested questions to get the conversation moving toward gap thinking:

- "If you were to rate your current provider on a scale of 1-10; 1 being awful and 10 being perfect, how would you rate them?"

- ○ If they answer, anything less than a 10, then you say, "What would it take for you to rate them a (2 numbers higher)?"
- "If your current supplier could be even better, what would have to happen?"
- "If you could draw this out perfectly, what would have to change?"
- "What does 'even better' look like?"
- "In a perfect world and under optimal conditions, what would this process look like?"

When your prospect starts discussing issues, challenges, *gaps*, etc....you should simply say these words: "I'm sure you said that for a reason. Would you mind telling me more?"

Remember, you are looking for a strategic entry point, a gap, which you can develop to justify your continued involvement with the account. Find a *gap* worth solving—this is how you help companies and people improve. If the improvement you describe creates a wide enough gap, then you'll gain a chance at moving to the next step.

Be Patient—Don't Jump into Sales Mode

You must resist the urge to switch gears from detective mode to sales mode. Stay in detective mode. Do not talk about your products at this stage. Stick to The EDGE and continue the steps in order.

EDGE selling is designed for you to focus on gaps. Even if there isn't a known gap, you're going to identify and develop a gap. Your gap could be a solution or option your buyer has never thought of, or even heard of. Hunt for gaps, expose them, then explain how other companies have benefited from taking action.

Every company has gaps, but not every company is willing to admit to having problems.

A Story of Finding a Gap

I had a new business prospect we had never done business with before. It was a huge bank in the Midwest, and I knew they had thousands of computers. Through dogged persistence and disciplined proactive stacking, I finally got in for a meeting. When I started going through The EDGE process, they told me, "You know what? We're good. We have all the technology we need right now. They work fine. We don't have any computer problems." I said, "Well, what are your biggest headaches when it comes to computing?" He said, "We really don't have any headaches."

If I had been using SPIN, that's where the conversation would have ended.

But I was using The EDGE. I quickly realized that because the decision maker didn't perceive any problems with their technology, I had to move on to look for a gap. I said, "Well, walk me through the process of how you get computers into your branches and get them set up and functioning."

This bank had 1,200 branches around the Midwest. He said, "Simple. We unpack them from their boxes, install our company software on each hard drive, and then ship them out to the branches."

"Why do you have them shipped here to headquarters before shipping them again to the branches?"

He said, "We have to install the software and make sure it's functioning and secure."

I realized that the customer didn't see any problem with that process; it's how they had always done it—but I spotted a gap. I said, "Help me understand this. So, eighty computers come in, your technicians leave whatever it is they're doing at the moment to unbox those computers, plug them into your server, download the software, and then re-box each computer and ship them out. How long does that take?"

"Oh, probably a couple hours per system," he responded.

Using the EDGE framework, I began developing the gap further: "You have to factor in the cost of shipping each computer twice, and the man hours it takes for your technicians to unpack and boot-up all those computers, install the software, and re-pack them. What's the hourly rate for those technicians? I bet it's not cheap. Do they get paid overtime? Is their department ever over budget because of all that overtime? What if you could eliminate that overtime, cut your shipping cost in half, and get your fully-configured computers to the branches faster? How much time, money, and risk would that save you?"

I could see the light bulbs going off in his head. He never saw a problem before. But now his mind was beginning to see the gap.

I continued and asked, "Imagine if you were able to install the software when the computer got built at the manu-facturing facility, and then just ship the computer from the facility directly to your branches?"

"I've never heard of that. You can do that?"

I said, "Yes. We custom-build everything we do, and we have a special group that can securely and safely install proprietary software right when we install the hard drive, so it's already done. It's tested, it goes out on UPS, and it works. How much time and money would that save you?"

He got out his calculator and started calculating the

cost and time savings. I could see the amazement in his expression.

With that extra step of developing the gap, the bank decided to give us a shot with a limited trial run. We did a pilot program and it worked flawlessly. They then gave me a deal for one hundred units. Again, it worked flawlessly. Within eight months, they decided they wanted to go with this new direct-ship system. I knew my competitors couldn't provide this service, so when the refresh went out to bid, guess who won this multi-year, multi-million-dollar piece of business? That's right, I did. And it wasn't because I had a better brand, better technology, or even a lower price—it's because I exposed a problem they didn't even know they had and saved them a *ton* of money.

That example demonstrates the key advantage of The EDGE system. If I had been using SPIN, I would have been shut down as soon as the buyer told me they had no problems. Using the EDGE, I was able to uncover a gap and show them how to make their situation even better. That bank deal turned out to be one of the biggest deals in the history of my division at that time.

G = GREATER GAP

I've been teaching The EDGE technique for years. At this

point, many gung-ho salespeople think they have grasped the key elements and are ready to start selling.

Not so fast. Be patient.

You have to move on to the G in EDGE—developing a greater gap. The goal of this step is to help the buyer realize and visualize both the potential negative outcome if they don't correct the gap, as well as the benefits if they do.

The future is an awesome force.

The best way to do this is with a technique called "future pacing." This is a skill that all top performing salespeople use to help customers see the impact of their actions or inactions six months or a year down the road. It works like this: you simply say, "Let's imagine we're six months down the road, you've continued to do things the same way you are now, and you've continued to deal with the frustrations and issues you've just discovered. What will happen if this doesn't get better?"

Help them visualize the repercussions of their problem getting significantly bigger down the road. How much money will this cost the company over the course of the next year? What will that do to their department's budget?

Next, you use future pacing to help the customer mentally

realize the benefits of actually making a change now. Say, "Now *imagine* it's six months in the future and you're not dealing with this problem anymore. Everything's working exactly as we described it. Your cost savings is showing up on the bottom line and you're able to reinvest that money into other areas of the business. You have happier employees. Your boss is happy with you. What's that going to mean for you?" The light will begin to show in their eyes as they picture the possibilities.

When you're building a greater gap, you're helping people imagine the beneficial outcome of making the change. You also have to build up the perceived negative repercussions of staying on the same course. Help the buyer see the worst-case scenario. Build it up to almost disastrous (but believable) proportions. If you do a good job here, even if your product carries a premium price, cost becomes less of an issue. Keep in mind, you really need to help them understand and emotionally experience the outcome. Top performers are great at framing the future in a way that decision makers can agree to. Average performers see deal after deal get stalled or lost because they haven't done this step properly.

Companies are in business to achieve a desired outcome. If you can help them achieve that outcome in a better, faster, and smarter way, you will have a higher chance of moving your opportunity forward.

E = EMOTIONAL CONNECTION THROUGH STORYTELLING

Here we've reached the final step in The EDGE method: creating an emotional connection. There's an old saying that is just as true today as it ever was:

> People buy emotionally, and then justify the decision with logic.

You might be tempted to think, "Well, I sell (name your widget). No one is buying these based on emotion." I disagree. People who say this haven't tried and adopted the methodologies that I teach in the EDGE process.

People Want to Make Safer Decisions—So Help Them

Every human has some level of emotion toward a big decision. Whether it's in their business or personal life, every significant decision carries an emotional connection with it. One of the most significant emotions surrounding decisions is fear, specifically fear of making the wrong decision. All buyers have this fear: "Am I doing the right thing here? I don't want to be sold to." To close big deals, you need a reliable process for minimizing that fear. The solution is *not* to pitch them by making them sit through an elaborate PowerPoint presentation about your company and the features and benefits of your products. The solution is *not* to use old-fashioned closing techniques to pressure them into signing. No one likes the feeling of being sold to. That destroys trust and can kill the deal. The solution is to lean into the rapport you've built, to be genuine and educated, and help them see past their fears to the benefits you're offering.

The Power of Storytelling

For this technique, it follows logically that you must actively collect, edit, write, and practice delivering a handful of powerful success stories, also called case studies. You want to pull these from either your own customers or from salespeople in your organization. The stories must be about real customers and they must be true. It helps if you can drop the name of the company when telling the story, but make sure you have permission, in writing, to use that companies name.

Collecting and writing these success stories may be a job for management and/or marketing, but the reps will have to help identify and collect the necessary details that are needed.

Here are the elements of a well-crafted sales case study: in its essence, a case study is simply a relatable story, well-told, that provides the ultimate value your existing clients are receiving based on working with you. Well-told stories are some of the most potent sales tools at your disposal. As with much of the strategies in this book, being an effective storyteller has a specific method for success:

Element #1. Keep it simple. The simple story is more successful than the complicated one. When we think of stories, it is often easy to convince ourselves that they have to be complex and detailed to be interesting. The truth is, however, that the simpler a story is, the more likely it will stick. Using simple language with low-complexity story lines is the best way to activate the brain regions that make us relate to the story.

Element #2. Every story does not have to be *your* story. You have marquis clients and recent wins in your office, region, or industry vertical. Take the time to understand the details of these successes. It's totally okay for you to share the details of clients and recent wins, even though you weren't part of them. You can say something simple to tee it up:

> One of our Directors, John Smith, is working with another client in your industry that was experiencing some of the same challenges you are. They too felt like they weren't receiving enough attention and were frustrated with the lack of proactive communication from their supplier. They turned to our company to solve their tough supply chain demands. They've been with us now for three years, and just renewed their

contract for another three years. They told us that their loyalty to us is because we actually live up to our product guarantees, which helps assure them that they are getting the advice they need to effectively secure their business, reduce risk, and have peace of mind. They know they can rely on us twenty-four hours a day.

Early in my speaking and consulting career, I used the stories of Tony Robbin's success or Chet Holmes success. Later, as I got my legs under me, I was able to share the stories of successes I was creating for my own clients.

Element #3. Use our template to help write your case studies. We developed the template specifically to make it easier for you to record and build a library of case studies. When you take a few minutes to fill in the template, you will have the foundational information to write, memorize, rehearse, and deliver your stories more effectively. You can download the free template at our website, www.SalesEDGEToolkit.com.

Element #4. Make sure the story is about a client, but don't use the client's name unless you have written permission. In a case where you don't have permission to use a client's name, give a simple description of the client: "One of our clients is the third largest manufacturing company in the United States." Describe the client in non-revealing ways, but always keep in mind that the client must be similar and relevant in some way to your prospect.

Element #5. Match the problems or issues described in the case study with similar problems or issues your prospect is experiencing. You might say something like, "They were experiencing the same problems as you. In fact, they told us that their former firm wasn't treating them like a priority client, had product glitches, had multiple installation issues, and weren't flexible in their overall approach and service. These are the same kind of issues you have described."

Element #6. Explain why the problems mattered so much. What impact did these issues have on your client? What happened as a result of their issues or dissatisfactions? Try saying something like, "This was causing them to have serious security concerns. Each time their former provider was needed for technical advice or support, they weren't able to help. The former firm also had high employee turnover, and this client had to spend precious time training the new company reps. This pulled valuable resources out of the field and led to a less safe environment."

Element #7. Explain why they chose your team and your product. What were their core reasons for picking you over other vendors? Any time you acquire a new client, it is always wise to ask them, "What is it that stood out about us that caused you to choose us?" Clients usually are comfortable telling you, and you can use their comments in your story.

Element #8. Describe what services you are performing for them. You should know which services you are performing for all your top clients. In some cases, when you reveal this, you may find that your prospective client wasn't even aware of all the services you are capable of performing for them, giving you a great opportunity to grow revenue with that same client.

Element #9. Finally, explain why your current clients are happy with you and use quantified numerical metrics whenever possible. Here are some questions you can ask yourself to gather these quantities:

- Exactly how much money, time, or other valuable resources did you save them?
- By what percentage did efficiency increase?
- How much did you decrease downtime?
- How much were they able to reduce their annual spend?
- Have they decided to renew their contract with you for another year, or more?
- Have they gone on to purchase multiple product lines through your company?

In this stage, you want to confidently be able to articulate that your client is not just happy, they are loyal to you.

Practice Your Storytelling

Ideally, your case study library will eventually contain twenty-plus well-written stories. Once you have your case studies collected, written, and edited, it's time to study and practice them. Memorize the stories and rehearse them. Learn them by heart so you can recite them at a moment's notice in a sales meeting. You never know when the situation will arise for you to insert your story in a way that is both persuasive and compelling for the listener. This will be time well spent and will lead to more sales and bigger deals.

"A well told story is the like the Ninja way of selling. It allows you to pitch what you do, without actually pitching."

If people feel like they're being pitched, they'll tune you out; but if you tell a story that subliminally connects with them, you will capture more of the minds of the people you are speaking with. People will never know that they're being pitched when you weave it into a good story.

Notice, at this point, I have yet to dive into the "how to deliver the details of your products and services." That is exactly what makes this different—if you're following what I teach, you should know by now that covering your features and benefits should be happening later in your process, not earlier.

In my opinion and experience, if you have completed all The EDGE steps, you are 70 percent of the way to winning a new client. Why? Because if they are talking with your competition, they likely are getting barraged with spec sheets, feature dumps, and pushy techniques.

My biggest pet peeves with salespeople:

- *Always talking and not asking questions*
- *Not listening. Maybe you are asking questions, but you are only listening to respond about how to sell something different.*
- *Listen to understand!*
- *Generic messages. Don't say things that give an impression that you are blessing me by talking to me.*
- *Stop looking for something and not having anything to offer (this happens with social media stuff).*
- *Know that it is YOUR CLIENT'S agenda that matters. Until you fully understand their problem, how can you give them a solution?*
- *You must understand me, then give me what I am looking for.*

—LARRY B., DIRECTOR OF TOOLS AND TECHNOLOGY

But *now* is still not the optimal time to start talking about what you can do to help them. To prepare yourself to win a *big* deal, you have to conduct a deeper dive into the prospects business.

Before you present a winning solution, another step is highly recommended—what we call "The Audit."

In the next chapter, I am going to show you exactly how to do that, and how to use the process to completely stand out from your competitors.

CHAPTER 8

BUILD YOUR STRATEGIC WIN PLAN

Success doesn't always come from innovation, it comes from flawless execution of a plan.

After you run your initial meetings, your next most important step is to start gathering pertinent client details to help you craft a compelling proposal that puts you into a position to win.

Oftentimes, this stage requires you to see more information—data, processes, reporting—and, depending on what you do, conduct site visits or interviews with specific people that will be involved with the decision process. These people may not be *the* decision makers, but their input will be key in how the decision makers decide what to do. These people are called Influencers.

THE CLIENT AUDIT

It is best to label this process. While we call it "The Audit," you might choose to call it a "deep dive" or even "discovery"—but, like an accounting firm, you ultimately want to look at as many details as possible to prescribe the most accurate recommendation.

When most people hear the word "audit," they start to cringe because they think of the IRS or an internal accounting audit. Relax. I'm talking about a client audit. This is one of the most powerful things you can do with a key account you're going after.

An audit means you earn permission to go in, review, understand, and diagnose the current processes and systems of the key accounts you're trying to sell. An audit will allow you to get all the information you need for your SWAP (Strategic Win Account Profile, which is outlined below). The audit helps you dive deeper into your prospect's business, so that you truly understand problems and gaps. You want to do an audit well in advance of presenting a solution.

When you do a client audit, it's like gaining the keys to the kingdom. You may walk through the building, meet people, have direct discussions with the plant supervisor, ask to see their processes, and look over their numbers and even their CRM data. An audit allows you to examine their business in a way that lets you focus on finding everything that can be improved with what they're doing now. If you do this right, you've gained permission to probe and explore to find those coveted problems, gaps, or missed opportunities for improvement.

HOW AN AUDIT CHANGED EVERYTHING

One of my clients sold commercial air filters and air handling products. Before I worked with them, they were selling primarily on price. They'd come into a prospective account, go straight to procurement, and say, "We sell air filters. What company are you buying from now?" The director of procurement would say, "I'll consider using your company, but you'll have to beat our current pricing. Here's the specs list of what we're buying and here's the price we're getting it at. Can you beat it?" The obvious problem was that it drives everyone's prices down and crushes profitability.

When this company learned about the EDGE, SWAP, and audits, it completely changed the way they sold, and they stopped making their primary point of entry through the procurement department. Now they meet with higher-level decision makers and set themselves up as industry experts and air handling consultants. In their initial meeting, their reps use The EDGE process to uncover problems and gaps. They say, "Before we even begin to discuss products or pricing, we first need to understand whether or not we can help you. Let us do a complete audit on your air handling systems. I'll bring in an air quality engineer. We'll run tests. We'll go through your buildings, and we'll come back and give you a detailed report of our findings. Fair enough?"

SELL THE AUDIT FIRST

Here's the key: *before* selling their solution, our client first sold the *audit*. By doing this, they built more trust, they were able to build rapport with more people, and they stood out from their competitors because, rather than just trying to sell filters, they sold their consultative advice first.

Once they had their prospect's approval, they walked through the facilities to find every gap imaginable. They developed those problems into urgent issues that were important to senior management and documented their findings in their online SWAP profile. By the time their reps got to the actual presentation phase, they were miles ahead of their competitors, and they set themselves up to be a true trusted resource.

Training your sales force on this one technique will radically transform the number of deals they win and have direct, positive impact on margins. Train your team to *first* close the prospect on the audit. Then have them use the audit/interviews to track what they learn during the process. This comes in very handy when it's time to present their solution proposal and justify pricing. The audit puts you in the best position to make a compelling case and explain why the prospect should change to your company.

RELATIONSHIP STRENGTHENING

Another key benefit of doing an audit is it allows you to strengthen your relationships with everybody involved at the prospect company. Be sure your team makes a good impression. Train your team members on the importance of building rapport. Don't take the rapport process for granted. Coach the people who are going to be doing the audit on-site with the client. Part of their job is to create likeability. Studies overwhelmingly show that we want to work with people we like, so they've got to be building rapport properly throughout the course of the audit.

One of my favorite tools to use when presenting the results of an audit is called the ROI calculator. Most companies don't use this. Where it makes sense, and once you have collected enough data during an audit, you can plug this data into a spreadsheet that calculates a predictable return on investment of making a change. This allows you to show the prospect quantitatively how making a change could benefit them. Show them you can save them money, reduce costs, save time, or increase their efficiency—ideally all of the above. This information helps you make the argument that spending more money for your product/ service will actually save them money in the long run. An ROI calculator demonstrates the quantifiable financial impact of switching to your company as a provider.

Great companies teach their teams how to perform effective audits. From building rapport to using the EDGE to creating the SWAP profile, your entire team should be trained in these crucial skills. It will profoundly impact your bottom line.

Use this process for your own team by going to www. salesedgetoolkit.com and downloading our "How to Conduct an Audit" document.

THE SWAP PLAN

Early in my career, I went into a sales meeting with a big client to give a presentation. I had a folder with me containing all the research I had done on the company— newspaper clippings, handwritten notes from previous meetings, printouts, sticky notes, industry statistics, and so on. I was really proud of all the great research I had collected. But the folder was a disorganized mess. As I got into the presentation, it was all over the map. Because my notes and research were disorganized, so was my presentation. I realized I had to figure out a repeatable system for capturing and organizing all my strategic account research and information.

I opened a Microsoft Word document on all my prospective and existing accounts and started tracking, typing, and organizing all information on that account in one place. I wanted the information to be centralized and organized. I realized that just doing this process helped me better understand the account, their needs, their gaps, and how to best approach them. When the time came for the big meeting or presentation, I was organized and prepared. I could recall the important information and conversations from previous meetings. I knew who their current supplier was, their current processes, what was working, and what their key issues were. And, because I knew this, I could build a strategic recommendation.

Over time, I organized and standardized the Word doc with categories to cover and incorporated prompts with key questions to ask. This helped me make sure nothing slipped through the cracks or got overlooked. That process was the beginning of what I now call the SWAP plan: a Strategic Win Account Profile.

THE NEED FOR SWAP

"Tactic without strategy is simply noise before the defeat"
—SUN TSU, ANCIENT CHINESE MILITARY STRATEGIST

You may have decent technical skill in executing tactics—getting meetings, writing proposals, delivering your pricing—but if you don't develop a big-picture account *strategy* for creating a compelling and winning presentation, you can expect to waste a lot of time.

Remember, *hope* is not a strategy in winning big accounts.

Having a SWAP helps salespeople define their strategy in advance and allows them to refine their strategy during the process. I built the process so that even a beginning salesperson can strategically go after new accounts in an organized, effective way. The SWAP profile tells you what you need to learn about each new account, whom you need to meet, what you need to discover, and what you need to review with the client. It provides a step-by-step guide and ultimately puts you in the best position to win.

If you follow the SWAP plan, by the time you get to the presentation phase, you will understand the client, each person involved, understand their issues and challenges, know who you are competing against, and clearly understand your prospect's goals and objectives. Then you can effectively match your solution to exactly what it is they're trying to accomplish and solve the problems that are preventing them from achieving their goals.

When you're hunting your ideal targets, you have to look at yourself like a detective. You and your team's job is to uncover all the clues needed to solve the mystery: how do you uniquely help this business achieve their goals in a better, faster, and smarter way by using your product/service as a key component of their success?

What would happen if all your salespeople took a strategic approach to going after the biggest and ideal clients in their territory?

Here are key baseline questions you *must* be able to answer that will put you in position to win:

- What are the higher order problems they need to solve?
- What problems do they have that they don't even realize they have?
- What process could be improved and would make sense for them to change?
- How does your recommendation positively effect money, risk, and time?

The SWAP process is a recipe for doing solid detective work. It makes sure nothing is overlooked.

ELEMENTS OF A SWAP PLAN

It's important to have all the key elements of SWAP plan:

#1. There should only be one document for each prospect. This gives you a single, central place to track the multiple conversations that will be required for you to fully understand your prospect. As stated earlier in this book, when you're hunting big deals there are an average of five to eight decision makers or influencers involved in the decision. Ideally, your detective work will include conversations with all of them. You may hear a different story from the head of purchasing and the VP of finance, so having notes of those conversations together will allow you to analyze and compare them.

There may also be multiple team members from *your* organization working on the account. As your team members contribute their findings at the end of the process, you'll have one centralized document that everyone can access, which allows you to build your winning case.

#2. Know that the SWAP is built for salespeople first and for management second. I didn't design SWAP to be like Salesforce.com or another traditional CRM. These mostly seem to be used by salespeople to track their daily activities, not necessarily to hunt big game. If your salespeople don't see value in working with a CRM or other system, they won't use it. Although we have integrated SWAP into many CRMs (including Salesforce.com), SWAP is just as effective as a stand-alone document.

Don't mistake your current CRM for a SWAP. SWAP is different. It is designed for one purpose—to help big game hunters go after huge deals and win them.

#3. The SWAP provides very specific direction; it's almost a paint-by-numbers approach. Here's why that's important. Bigger deals are more complex, the sales cycle is longer, and you will have more meetings, more research, and more data points to keep track of. The SWAP provides a consistent tracking system. What matters is not just that you have a meeting with key people, but that you know what to ask them and then record and analyze that information. SWAP will prompt you to ask the right questions in the right order, so they will ultimately understand the totality of the organization and the key factors that matter to each decision maker. By the end, you'll know if there is a business problem worth solving, who your competitors are, who is going to be at the buyer's table, and you will have a well-crafted message strategy to cause you to stand out from the pack.

BUILD YOUR SWAP PROFILE

Step #1. Create a big-picture situational overview. This is very basic information that you can find online: name of the company, key management, industry trends, number of employees, annual revenue, number of locations, business structure, competitors, suppliers, and so on. Spend time on Google and LinkedIn, then collect your findings in SWAP. Dig as deep as you can to learn about who their current suppliers are and how they're doing. Use this information to start thinking about problems you might be able to solve and gaps that might exist. What is your unique solution to reduce risk, to save money, or increase efficiencies? You'll look for ways to develop these gaps once you get inside the account.

> Remember, no gap means no sale. You must be able to show that the pain of staying the same is greater than any perceived pain of change.

Step #2. Identify everyone who's involved in the decision-making process. This is referred to as "The Buyer's Table." This could be everyone from the C-suite to the project managers, the division directors, and the subject matter experts (SMEs). It could also include influencers from outside the company—a consultant, legal counsel, agency, etc.

Your goal when you identify their decision-making team—called the Buyer's Table—is ultimately to match up *your* selling team with *each member* of the buying team. You want your technical specialist talking to their technical specialists. You want your finance people talking to their finance people. You want your senior people talking to their senior people. There's immense power in team-based selling, but you have to match your experts with their experts.

Let's examine some the typical personas that will be at your Buyer's Table:

- **The Ultimate Decision Maker (UDM).** This is the person who can say yes without asking anyone else. This isn't always the CEO or president. Regardless of their title, you should always know who ultimately will approve/sign the deal.
- **The Executive Sponsor.** This person is often referred to as the "Internal Coach" and is someone you have a deeper relationship with in comparison to the rest of the people at the buyer's table. Your Executive Sponsor is one of *the* most important people as it relates to winning new business. These people typically want *you* and your team involved with them and their team.
  - The *major* benefit of the Executive Sponsor is that they will tell you what is going on behind the scenes. They'll be the person who calls you (offline) to tell you what is being said in the meetings you are not in, how your competition is positioning themselves, which of their team members may be problems for you, and sometimes, they will tell you exactly where you need to be in terms of pricing, to win the deal.
- **Subject Matter Experts (SMEs).** These people have

a variety of titles and their role is to oversee the viability of your (and your competitors) solutions as they apply to their company. These are usually the technical people who are going to test what you do and provide a technical opinion toward making the right choice for their company.

- **Senior Financial Influencer.** This is typically the Senior Financial person, who is responsible for contract negotiation, terms of the deal, and service level agreements (SLAs). They are typically the CFOs, Senior Procurement Specialists, or Finance Managers.
- **Other Influencers.** These are people who have a "seat at the table" and will have influence on the final decision. These may be consultants, external experts, or key people that the UDM has trust and respect for.
- **Blockers.** These are the people who *don't* want you and your company to win. Sometimes these people have a better relationship with a competitor. Sometimes they favor your competitor's uniqueness over yours, and sometimes they were the people who originally recommended the current, and unsuccessful solution. Blockers always exist. Not to think so is naïve. In the old Western movies, they'd say, "The bullet that you *don't* see is the one that kills you." Don't let a blocker behind the scenes stop your deal in its tracks.

Note: Usually, your Executive Sponsor will inform you of the Blocker. Use your relationship with the Executive Sponsor to help understand your Blocker's concerns, and even better, get you some direct facetime with your Blocker to help alleviate any issues they may perceive as not in your favor.

Additional note on Blockers: One of the best ways to alleviate fears with these people is not by the words you say, but by layering them with social proof. Proof in the form of documentation such as case studies. Or, if they're concerned about change, show them successful transition plans that worked well in other companies. Show them the biographies of your transition team. Show them proof of other companies and brands that switched to you and are glad they did.

In extreme cases, you could even ask one of your existing clients to call the blocker on your behalf to help alleviate their concerns. You have to go to every possible level to handle the Blocker's objections, otherwise you could lose the deal. Handling Blockers is one of the most valuable things you can spend your time on. Failing to take them seriously can cost you dearly.

You must be able to talk the talk. Bring in your experts who can understand what my business problem is. You and your team must resonate with that.

—LARRY B., DIRECTOR OF TOOLS AND TECHNOLOGY

Step #3. Build Your Selling Team. Engaging a buying team is about meeting their needs, not your needs. This is why you need to build your selling team based off the buyer's table team members. There is nothing worse than having your sales guy trying to answer detailed technical questions being asked by the prospect's chief engineer. That is an obvious recipe for disaster. Or, let's imagine that the Senior Financial Influencer is negotiating price, shipping, quantity discounts, or other preferences, and the salesperson has to constantly call someone else in order to get approvals. Another recipe for disaster.

It is essential that one of the main roles of the professional salesperson is to build their selling team *after* identifying the personnel involved at the Buyer's Table.

Bottom line: if you want to win big deals, *never* send a salesperson alone.

Step #4. Identify and Build Your Strategic Message. After you've interviewed key people and done research at the company, it's time to start focusing in on your strategic message. What is your strategic message and ultimate strategy? If it's solving a known problem, then you need to research information that will help you develop the consequences of that problem not being solved. If there is no known problem, your strategy will focus around developing opportunities to make the current situation even better. Ultimately, to win the big deals, there is *always* a theme, a strategy, and a series of focus points that cause you and your company to stand out.

LOOK FOR THE FOG

I'm a big fan of the book *Whale Hunting* by Tom Searcy. He says that during your client conversations you need to be constantly looking for the FOG:

The F stands for facts. The facts are usually what everyone—including your competitors—will already know. The facts are important and are usually laid out in an RFP or RFI, but are not as important as the O and the G.

The O stands for opinions. When you meet with each buying team member, try to understand what his or her opinions are of the current supplier, issues with the current process, and their candid thoughts on the overall situation. One person may be totally unaware of something that is obvious to another. To understand opinions, ask the following questions:

- What are your thoughts on this?
- What impact does this have on your division?
- How does this affect the way you do your job?
- Are you happy with the current situation?
- NOTE: Make sure you document and track each conversation.

The G stands for gossip. Gossip can be very valuable when hunting big game. There are all kinds of gossip. Are any of the decision makers retiring or getting ready to leave the company? Is anyone about to get promoted or demoted? Gossip can have a big impact on whether you win the deal, so it's worth uncovering.

The best way to find out the inside scoop and what's going on in the rumor mill is during conversations outside of the office. Meet some of your contacts within the company for drinks after hours. Or speak to them on their cell phone.

If you're actively looking for facts, opinions, and gossip you will find it. You'll never find what you're not actively looking for. The more of the FOG you have, the better you can craft your ultimate strategic positioning.

Step #5: Clearly identify, define, and understand the customer's decision-making process, as well as their timeline. If you can list the values and criteria they use to make buying decisions, you'll be far ahead of the competition. This is critical to determining your overall account strategy.

To get information on their decision-making process, ask the following questions:

- How did they decide last time?
- Describe the typical process for making a decision like this.
- What are the key criteria they will be judging their decision on? This could be quality of products/service, relevant experience, price, flexibility, delivery details, etc.
- Why and how did they choose the last provider?
- Why didn't they select you last time?
- Who, of the decision-making team, has the most influence?
- Who has the final say?

MAKE SURE YOU'RE USING ONLINE RESOURCES

When you're hunting big game, you have to take some extra steps. Set up a Google alert so you can track any news stories (or trigger events) that pop up about your key targets. Also connect and keep track of all of them on LinkedIn. These resources will often alert you to key events taking place at your target company in real time. You should do this for your existing clients as well. Utilize technology to stay informed about the latest news on your prospects.

Your Sales Hunting strategy is ultimately a specific set of planned behaviors and techniques your company needs to master in order to create a competitive advantage.

Having few contacts in a company, no detailed strategic plan, no message strategy, and no understanding of the prospects needs, pain, or ultimate desires is a recipe for putting in a lot of hours to win the deal that has little to no return.

By executing the details of your Strategic Win Account Plan, you're putting yourself in the very best position to win.

But you still don't have the deal yet. You have to build a powerful, persuasive, and compelling presentation designed to create consensus from your Buyer's Table.

Let's get started.

CHAPTER 9

BUILDING YOUR WINNING PRESENTATION

"You have come this far to just come this far"

Now that you've gotten to this stage, your next step is to build and deliver a compelling and *winning* presentation. Don't take this step lightly. If you are truly on a level playing field with the competition, this is going to be your *one shot* at standing out and becoming the obvious choice above your competition.

WHAT *NOT* TO DO

There is a common problem with almost all presentations I see. Let me explain:

It's likely that your presentation is mostly boiler plate, and largely spends time discussing *you*—your company, your history, the client brands you work with, and why you are the best. How do I know this? Because that's what just about every company does. I've been in sales consulting for a long time, and I've seen this pattern hundreds of times. Every company gives basically the same sales presentation, and then they can't understand why the clients look bored to tears and half asleep.

INTERVIEW WITH A BUYER

Do not come in and show me a bunch of shitty PowerPoint slides. You will be dismissed fast.

—MIKE S., VP OF PRODUCT MANAGEMENT AND MARKETING

But just know that if you do the kind of presentation described above, the same kind of presentation your competitors will surely be doing, you are jeopardizing your opportunity to win. If your presentation looks and sounds like all your competitors, in the buyer's mind, the only differentiating factor is price. We all know how that movie ends.

I wrote earlier in this book that a premium price requires a premium story. Well, a premium price also requires a premium presentation. That's what this chapter is all about.

Presentations are incredibly important at this stage in

the sales cycle; deals can be won or lost here. If the buyer sees you and your competitors as equals, the group that presents more effectively and more persuasively will win more often. You can increase your batting average by paying attention to this phase of the selling process and following the steps in this chapter.

Let's get into the details

THE POWER OF VISUAL AIDS

A question I often get is, "Do I have to use a PowerPoint?" The answer is absolutely yes; if you have the option, *always* choose to present with slides. If where you are presenting doesn't accommodate that, at the bare minimum have your presentation printed out and hand copies to everyone at the buyer's table. Then go through it slide by slide. Without the use of slides and visual aids, you can miss leveraging all the visually stimulating impact points of your story.

Independent research backs up what I've concluded on my own. I've watched countless sales presentations, both with and without slides. It has been said that eighty-five percent of information that reaches the brain comes through the eyes. There is a tremendous difference between presenting a visual slide deck, versus just handing a contract to someone and watching them flip through the pages and go straight to the price. If they do that, you're in serious danger of losing. In other words, if your audience doesn't get the context of what you're offering, especially if you are a higher price, then you have less chance of standing out.

Your presentation needs to be visually rich. Avoid plain text on a white background at all costs. Every slide should have a graphic and every graphic should be strategically chosen for each slide. The graphic can determine the emotion around a slide. Some of the best graphics are pictures of faces that display emotion—happiness, concern, frustration, worry. Pick your graphics and images strategically to match the message and tone you want to convey with each slide.

PRESENTATION CONTENT

What content should you include in your presentation? Essentially, you want to recap everything you've learned about the client during your research and audit: their goals, their issues and problems, what they could be doing better that would help them meet or exceed their goals faster and more efficiently.

Then, you want to be able to show proof that you can do what you say you're going to do. You've got to be able to communicate your ultimate difference that makes the difference. And every great presentation ends with a stellar executive summary. The executive summary portion is designed so that people will look at it and realize choosing you is an easy decision.

In addition to the executive summary, there are some signature slides that you should always have in your deck.

START WITH THE COVER PAGE

The cover page is that first slide they look at as you're introducing yourself. As you begin presenting, the audience will glance from you to the cover slide and back to you. You want that slide to begin influencing what they're thinking about you and how they're going to perceive your message. The cover slide should give a very distinctive *benefit* your organization will deliver for the client. How you can help the client achieve more, spend less, reduce risk, increase productivity, decrease waste, etc. There should always be a compelling benefit that is specific to the client on the cover slide.

If you have performed The EDGE Process and built your SWAP, you should know what your prospects' ultimate goals are. Your cover page should say something like, "Helping you achieve (their desired goal)."

THE AGENDA SLIDE

The agenda slide is critical because, by setting the agenda, you are in control of the meeting. The agenda should not be more than six points. Your agenda lays out what you are about to cover and sets the tone for the rest of the meeting.

DIAGNOSTIC OVERVIEW SLIDE

Next, is an overview of the diagnostic work you've done in your audit. Describe all the research and information you've collected, the people you've met with, what you've studied, what you've read, what you've looked at, and explain how you did your audit. This slide proves you've done your homework and know this area of their business, and it allows you to justify the recommendation you're about to make. For example, you might say something like:

> We've met with several members of your team, reviewed your current processes, studied your key reports for the last three years, walked through every one of your sites, had our engineers do an assessment, done site surveys, and we've even had dialogue with some of your customers...

GOALS ALIGNMENT SLIDE

The next slide is called an alignment slide, which talks about their goals and demonstrates that you understand what they are trying to accomplish. Don't just *say* you understand their goals; effectively communicate that you and your organization are *in alignment* with their goals. You might say something like,

> As a result of our research and based on what you've told us, your goals are the following: you want to:

- reduce your overall spend
- reduce your overall risk
- increase the efficiency of your employees
- improve your employee satisfaction scores
- reduce the time it takes to ship product

At this point, you are only four slides into the presentation, but you're going to start to see heads nodding around the conference table if you do this right. They're beginning to see that you understand their needs and are aligned with their goals. They believe that you "get" them and their company.

PROBLEMS AND ISSUES SLIDE

Slide number four lists the problems, issues, and dissatisfactions discovered in your audit. This is an important slide and is the basis for the recommendations you're about to give. You have to be strong enough in this slide to convincingly lay out that you've discovered the issues that will keep them from achieving the goals listed in the previous slide.

The sweet spot is about four to six key issues. If you haven't gone through The EDGE process, you haven't prepared your strategic win account profile, and you haven't been astute at really understanding the gap between where they are and where they want to be, then you've lost all mojo in this presentation.

PROBLEM EXPLORATION SLIDES

The following four to six slides will explore each of those problems in greater detail. Lay these out using one slide per problem. With these, you're going to demonstrate specifically how you solve for the client each of the problems you've identified. Each slide will describe the problem, the solution, and the benefits that you bring them to solve the issues.

Understand that by simply doing this style of presentation, you are going to be well ahead of other vendors. Most of them are going to come in with a presentation about how great their own company is, their big clients, and way too many details about their speeds and feeds. That is, if they give a formal presentation at all. In contrast, your entire presentation is about *them* and *their company*. Not about *you* and *your company*. Keep your focus on them.

THE TRANSITION SLIDE

The next step is crucial. You must do a thorough job of explaining the transition process. After all, you are asking them to make a big change, or to choose you to help them with a desired change. Some people naturally fear change. You have to *show* them that you've done this numerous times and that you'll make sure it goes smoothly. If you fail to convince them of this, you may lose the deal. Whatever your system is, you've got to articulate it in a graphical way on a slide.

You might say, "We know change can be scary. So, we have a five-step transition process that we've perfected over countless installs. It has been honed to minimize any disruption for our clients. It will secure your data and ensure a seamless switchover process."

Most sales teams miss this piece completely. Know that this hidden objection can kill the deal. You want to discuss your "smooth transition process" as clearly and confidently as possible.

THE PROOF SLIDE(S)

Now that you've set this piece up, you have to go into what are called your "proof" slides.

The first proof slides will be case studies. These are

important, and if you lay them out right visually, they allow you to effectively pitch without actually pitching.

FIVE KEY ELEMENTS OF A CASE STUDY SLIDE

Element #1. In the first bullet point, describe your client and their business. Only use the company's name if you have permission. If you don't have permission, then use a vague description, such as, "Another large manufacturing firm in Southern California." If you can get permission to use their name and logo, you've got a tool that will help solidify and validate your presentation.

Element #2. List the issues, problems, and challenges they were experiencing.

Element #3. Tell why they chose you over the competition: "They went through a similar process, they looked at us and all of our competitors, and they chose us because they trusted us, because of our industry knowledge, and because of our expertise in their industry."

Element #4. Describe what products or services of yours they are using.

Element #5. In the last bullet point, describe their results. What quantifiable benefit did the client receive? You have to articulate the specific results that your clients are getting as a result of working with you. The more quantified, the better.

As an added benefit, offer them the opportunity to call the senior person you are working with at that company to interview them about your performance. *Nobody*, including your competitors, is doing this.

"YOUR TEAM" SLIDE

After you've gone through your case study, incorporate slides that introduce and sell *your* engagement team members. Your engagement team is made up of the people who are going to work intricately with the new customer. This is another area that most organizations miss. The phrase you want to use in this part of the presentation is, "Look, great relationships always boil down to the level and quality of people who are involved on a day-to-day basis. Let me introduce you to your engagement team."

At this stage, you're going to introduce everybody who is going to be involved—customer service reps, managers, systems engineers, etc. You want to describe each one of them and show their picture, if possible. You can't just say it's going to be Robert, Sue, Kim, and Jonathon. You've got to sell the merit of the team they will be working with.

This is the one point in the presentation where you *actually do sell*. You have to sell their professional background. You have to describe how great they are, and not just at their jobs. Maybe you exemplify something about them personally: "Paul has been the leader of his local Boy Scout troop for twenty-two years. He's a former Eagle scout, and he was a straight-A student. You're going to love working with Paul."

You want to exemplify in four to six bullets the absolute key professional and (some) personal highlights of the individuals involved, because oftentimes companies will pick you just because they like your team better. If you miss this opportunity to sell the backgrounds and bios of your team members, you risk losing this deal. Most of your competitors will not know or take the time to build that personal and professional connection between their prospective client and their own team.

ABOUT YOUR COMPANY SLIDE

Then, the second to last slide is about you and your company. Clearly note, this slide is at the *end* of your presentation, not the beginning. But now that you're finally talking about yourself, feel free to brag a little bit: "We've been in business for twenty-five years. We've won six industry awards, and we have thirty locations." If possible show some of the other relevant brands you work with. But the key is to talk about your company at the end of the presentation, *never* at the beginning. And keep it short. If you have gotten this far, they have already vetted you.

EXECUTIVE SUMMARY SLIDE

The final slide is a strong, concise executive summary. Why is the executive summary so important? Because of something called the law of remembrance. Studies show that people remember most how you ended, second most how you started, and they remember least what was in the middle.

The executive summary reiterates why you're the best choice. This is where you distinctly lay out all your "differences that make the difference." By choosing you, how will that prospect organization achieve their business results and solve their problems? You have to state it in the form of a "future paced" benefit:

- You will achieve...
- You will receive...
- You will benefit from...
- You will reduce...
- You will have faster...
- By choosing us, you will receive all the following benefits that you said you wanted...

**Special note: Depending on your industry, be smart on the claims that you make in the Executive Summary. Know that when you say: "By choosing us you will achieve..." whatever you say will be the expectation in terms of executing the contract. As an example, when a former client of ours was in the accounting field, we could not say "You will benefit from..." due to legal reasons. We simply changed the language to say: "You MAY benefit from..." So, use your language patterns wisely.

The presentation techniques in this chapter have been used to close hundreds of millions, if not billions of dollars-worth of deals. Do not take shortcuts at this stage. You've worked so hard to get here, don't repeat the mistake that most companies make by leaving your presentations to chance. Pay attention to every fine detail, follow this process, and watch your results continue to grow. By sticking to the process in this chapter, you'll soon be winning more deals, winning bigger deals, and not getting caught in the vice grip of lowest price wins.

WHY THIS WORKS

Why will you have such a tremendous increase in wins by using this presentation? Because most of your competitors will give a presentation that talks about themselves. Their deck may have fancy graphics and look nice, but it likely doesn't talk about anything the prospect actually cares about. Remember, your prospect company only cares about what you can do for them. At this stage in the game, they don't care as much about your company history, although you will mention that at the end.

PLAY TO WIN!

When you show up and deliver a powerful presentation focused entirely on the prospect, you set yourself up to be the obvious choice.

Here are your keys:

- You communicate what research you've done
- You align with their goals
- You identify the problems that you solve for them
- You show how you solve them
- You layer your solutions with proof by including two case studies
- You discuss your amazing team members who will serve them
- You spend a brief time on the About Us slide
- You have a compelling Executive Summary slide

Being different is better than being better. If your competitors seem to be the same as you (in the client's mind), it's your presentation that is going to make all the difference in the world.

Now that you've built a presentation that will cause you to stand out, the next step is imperative. You have to be prepared to *deliver* an outstanding presentation. The next chapter will show you how to "wow" your audience, even if you don't love public speaking—so keep reading.

CHAPTER 10

DELIVERING A WINNING PRESENTATION

What you present is important. **How** *you present it will make all the difference in the world.*

—GENE MCNAUGHTON

How you deliver a presentation is as important as what you deliver. You can have the greatest slide deck in the world, but if you show up unprepared, unrehearsed, or you look like a robot reading every word of every slide, you'll have wasted all the time and effort you spent preparing to win the account—whether you're presenting in-person or on a webinar.

Early in my career, I gave one of the worst presentations ever. It was so horrible that, if I hadn't been the speaker,

I would've walked out on myself! To make matters worse, there were about two hundred people in the room watching. As soon as I got up to speak, I looked into the crowd and panic gripped me. I got a bad case of cotton mouth, and I didn't have any water at the podium. Soon, I could barely breathe. My knees began to shake. It's called *terror*!

After that humiliating experience, I was determined never to go through something like that again. I became a student of public speaking. I took classes. I read books. I got back in the game and began finding every chance to speak that I could. I took it seriously. I also became a student of great speakers. By studying the art and craft of public speaking, over time I began to understand what makes the difference between an effective presentation and a mediocre one.

LESS THAN NATURAL

Speaking is like any other skill—practice makes perfect. Think about a sport, golf for example. No one is born a great golfer. First, you must have an interest in golf. You also have to take lessons to learn the basics, work on your craft, and study people who are world-class golfers. Then you have to practice, knowing that you will make mistakes along the way. Great golfers make it look easy, but we all know it isn't.

The same is true with speaking and presenting. It's a

learned skill that anyone can master. You just have to commit to it.

> Public speaking has been one of the most profitable skillsets I have ever developed.

In this chapter, you'll learn how to *prepare* and *deliver* a highly persuasive presentation using simple steps to help you be in your best shape professionally and psychologically—*before* you walk in the room to set up.

Let's face it, many of you are presenting today, performing internal or external presentations, but most have had little to no presentation training. This short chapter will help you with the basics, and help you reduce the uncomfortable experience of nervous energy.

PREPARE...BEFORE THE NIGHT BEFORE

When it comes to presentation time, if you think about it, most salespeople—in all industries—are usually cramming the presentation together the night before, using versions of old PowerPoints with pictures that are likely outdated. Then, the morning of the presentation, if you are presenting as a group, you look at each other and say, "Okay, you do the first ten slides, you do the second section of slides, you do the third section of slides." And then they feel prepared!

Now you tell me, does that sound like a group of people ready, psychically and emotionally, to persuade an audience to choose them over a competing company? I don't think so.

Now, in contrast, let's look at what you could and *should* be doing prior to your next presentation:

1. One of the first steps is knowing when the presentation is and how much time you have. You want to reverse engineer your time frames, so you give yourself time to review and practice your presentation. This serves you in two ways: (a) it allows you plenty of time to practice, and (b) it gives you time to go through your presentation with a fine-toothed comb and make sure there are no obvious errors, including spelling and grammatical errors. But don't wait until the last minute!

2. Decide in advance which members of your sellers' team will speak. As a friendly reminder: always work to make sure you have the right people on your team to match the buyer's table team. In other words, if one of the buyer's team members asks a tricky question, you want your best expert there to have the answer on the spot.

3. Practice well—at least three times together (or by yourself). Notice I said the word "together." That's for a reason. The more you practice the presentation as a team, the better you get. You get better at setting

up the next slide and the next person; you get better at the hand off, and it shows great professionalism in front of the client.

Remember, practice doesn't make perfect, practice makes permanent.

DELIVERY DAY "NO-BRAINERS"

Finally, there are your "day of the presentation" suggested rituals. While some of these are simple, let me give you a little reminder:

- **Get a good night's sleep.** There are a number of studies that show the importance of sufficient sleep. If this presentation means a lot to you and your team members, go to bed early to help your physical presentation.
- **Eat a healthy breakfast.** Today is not the day to use the buffet. Remember, you want your body to be in its peak state while you are in front of that buyer's table. Be smart about what you are putting into your body in the morning. Remember, too much caffeine can cause you to be even more nervous during presenting time, so keep it simple and watch your intake.
- **If you present in the afternoon, review your presentation multiple times in the morning.** If you have the option, get together with the presenting team ahead

of time and do a full walk-through. Yes, I mean every person presenting out loud, in front of each other.

- **If you eat before your presentation, use nourishing food, but do not go in front of a group with a full stomach.** If you're full, it'll impact your breathing and throw off your overall presentation. Think about what it feels like after a nice Thanksgiving meal, then walking up a flight of steps...it's hard to breathe! Breathing is critical when it comes to speaking well. My rule of thumb is to go in nourished, but slightly hungry.

- **Get there thirty minutes in advance (if possible).** This will allow you to make sure that all of your audio/visual equipment is plugged in and working. Never forget Murphy's Law that says, "Something could always go wrong, so plan for it."

- **Always bring your presentation on a flash drive as a backup.** You never know whether a client will want you to present from their computer or yours, and what if your PC has a problem?

- **Have all your pre-handouts (forms, printouts, etc.) on the desk, prior to the client walking in.** This shows that you are prepared and professional.

- **Think through who on your team is going to sit where.** It's best to have the presenting team sitting closer to the front of the room. It makes it easier to get them in front of the room. If you are bringing additional team members, have them sit toward the back, but don't forget to introduce them.

THE POWER OF STATE MANAGEMENT

Now, finally, you've made it this far—it's presentation time.

As mentioned earlier, "You've come this far to just come this far"—now it's go time!

The most important point about "go time" is to make sure you manage your physical and emotional state. There's nothing worse than a low energy presenter who clearly shows nervous energy. In fact, if you were to deliver that way, even the GREATEST presentation in the world, the most well-crafted deck ever—will deflate immediately. Let's make sure that never happens for you.

There are three keys to putting yourself into a "state of readiness" right before you walk in a room.

FIRST IMPRESSIONS ARE EVERYTHING

One thing to remember is that people start forming impressions about you—not when you step up to speak— but the actual minute you've walked into the room. You want to prepare yourselves to walk in the room with absolute certainty and confidence.

By this stage, you have planned and prepared an awesome presentation. You have reviewed it multiple times to assure that it is error free. You have decided well in advance who is going to say what and have practiced your presentation out loud, together, multiple times. You have timed it out so you stay on track and stay within your given time frame. You have decided strategically who is going to sit where, your materials are laid out, and you've double checked your PowerPoint connection and the clicker. You are minutes from delivering a huge win for you and your company.

What else can you do? Well, now it's time to get yourself into a physical and mental state to deliver your brilliance. This comes in three simple steps:

1. **Clarify and see your ultimate outcome.** We've all heard about the power of visualization, but I'm asking you to truly visualize the audiences' heads nodding, their expressions smiling, and a general look of happiness on their faces. You have helped them choose the winning company (you and your team), and you are going to help them, better than anyone, achieve their goals. I know this sounds a bit hokey, but it works. See your ultimate outcome in advance, visualize your audience in full agreement, and imagine them being proud of the presentation you have prepared for them.

2. **Practice positive self-talk.** What do you think about right before you present? Does nervousness ever show up? If so, that's ok; in fact, it is NORMAL. I recommend that you use this time to re-remind yourself

of how fully you prepared, how well you know your presentation, that you have practiced well, and that you are going to deliver better than any other company they will see.

Use some language like "*I got this! I deserve to win this one! They are going to LOVE this presentation!*" Say that over and over again.

Self-talk is everything and will help you "dance" with any nerves you may have.

3. **Manage your physiology.** Know this—**motion creates emotion**. Before you go in front of the room, I recommend that you step off to the side or into the hallway (or even while you're still in the elevator) and *stretch* your body out. I know this sounds a little weird, but it makes a TON of difference. You can jump up and down, twist your back, touch your toes, stretch your hamstrings. Do something, *anything* that gets your blood flowing, so that when you walk in, you walk in with **energy**. There is nothing worse than a low energy presentation. By using this simple method (stretching, moving your body), you will immediately increase your blood flow and your energy.

When you walk into a room completely prepared, in command of a well-laid-out presentation, with great confidence and in peak physical condition—half of your battle is won even before you start showing your presentation.

Remember, you will always get rewarded in public for the things you practice the most in private. This is a key area to practice.

Prepare, practice, and present to win!

PART FOUR

WINNING, KEEPING, AND GROWING YOUR ACCOUNTS

CHAPTER 11

MOVING YOUR DEAL FORWARD

If you've done the work—you've followed the guidance in the previous pages, built massive rapport, done the right research, and delivered a compelling presentation—all about them and not about you. You have solved their problem or shown them a better path to achieve their goals. At this stage, if you've done all of this, you deserve to win. The steps outlined in these chapters have led you to this moment. Your competitors aren't likely following these disciplines, and that puts you way ahead of the curve.

What you do from here is crucial to what happens next. I'm sure you've heard the saying, "Slow down to speed up." If you want to close the deal, throw this mantra out the window. Now is the time to speed up! Don't drag your feet. Don't give them time to "think it over and get back to you." It's your time to stand out, pull even further ahead, and bring this deal home.

THE WAITING GAME

At the end of a presentation, you may shake the client's hand, exchange some nods, and hear, "Thank you for your time. We appreciate all the work you put into this. You should be hearing from us within the next two weeks."

You wonder, *what happens now?* How do you confidently move this deal forward?

Unfortunately, the real world doesn't often offer your deals served to you on a silver platter. They rarely have a neat and clean ending. Many deals require a little more legwork. The client often won't get back to you right away with an answer. There may be a delay for one reason or another. For them, it's a big decision. One they don't intend to take lightly.

Many salespeople, at this point, stop everything and go into waiting mode. They check their voicemail eight times a day. They aggressively stare at their inbox hoping to see an incoming message that says, "Congratulations!" Soon they start to play head games with themselves. "Did I do something wrong? What did I miss? Was the competition better than we were?"

> Know this: time kills deals. Do not play the waiting game.

I recommend that you do not play the waiting game. Now is the time to take massive action.

You must implement a proactive strategy and stand out among your peers. When a deal stalls and you haven't heard back, there is a set course of action you must take.

Your first steps should focus on being top of mind as they make their final decision. This doesn't mean going overboard, calling multiple times per day, sending emails and leaving voicemails for each person that was at the buyer's table. What it does mean is that you want them to know they are your number one priority, that their business is important to you, and that you are going to be available to give them the quality of service you represented in your presentation.

It's completely acceptable to call them before their indicated time frame—that is unless you have been told otherwise. Pick up the phone and call your key contact within the organization. If they answer, simply say you wanted to check in on the status of the decision, and you're available to add any clarifications they may need. If you are sent to their voicemail, leave a message to that effect. If you don't get a callback after a day or two, write the same message in an email. You are not going to sit passively by. You are there to earn their business.

You worked hard on this deal and you deserve to hear from them.

HOW TO UNSTICK STUCK DEALS

As mentioned earlier in this book, one of the smartest sales strategists I have ever met in my life is Tom Searcy, author of the book *Whale Hunting*. I learned a ton from this guy, not just in reading his books, but in listening to him speak, watching his videos, and getting to know him personally. He was the first person I ever heard use the phrase "stuck deals." I always recommend his books, if you are a big deal hunter.

KEYS TO MOVING YOUR DEALS FORWARD

The problem comes when you've left several messages and sent emails yet there's still no response. People who used to call you back, aren't any more. They're not responding.

This is what is called a stuck deal, and there are many reasons this can happen:

- The decision makers could disagree on which vendor to go with, so they're still hashing it out and comparing proposals.
- The buyer's table has a few more important questions that they forgot to ask each vendor/firm during the

presentations, which means they have clarifications to discuss with you.

- The Ultimate Decision Maker is confused and can't decide, which often ends with the them not making *any* decision and staying with the status quo. You can't let that happen.

The way to push a stuck deal forward is to start by looking backward at what you've done up until this point.

#1. Review your SWAP profile. Did you follow the steps? Did you take good notes? Did you develop problems or gaps? Did you have relationships with the right people? Did you establish and understand the higher order business problem and show them how you and your team could help them at the highest levels?

#2. Compare your SWAP profile to the presentation that you delivered. Were there any key elements from the SWAP profile you left out? Did you accurately convey an understanding of the company and their gaps? Did you present a valid solution? Did your solution help them meet their organizational goals? Did you deliver killer case studies that matched up to what your prospect is trying to do? Try to objectively assess how well you did in these areas and whether you were weak in spots or missed anything important. You are trying to identify any parts of your presentation that could have potentially stalled the decision. And if you do, you can take action.

#3. Leverage your best contacts inside the company. Ask yourself these questions:

- Are you truly working with an executive sponsor or internal coach? Is there someone on the inside you've built a really strong relationship with who can tell you what's really going on?
- Do you have a relationship with the person who is the ultimate decision maker? Are you able to call and ask for an update on where the decision process is right now?
- Is there anyone else at the company you can call who might know where the deal stands?
- Are you clear on who's problems you are really solving? Who are your advocates within the client company?
- To make sure you are thinking about this the right way, make sure you understand:
    - Who at the buyer's table—which person's division or department—has the most to lose if they *don't* make a change because you don't win this opportunity.
    - Who at the buyer's table has the most to gain if you *do* get the deal.
- Is there a blocker at the buyer's table you haven't properly handled and whose concerns you haven't

addressed? Ask if you can come in and meet with them. Then remind them of the problems you've discovered, what implications those problems have, and how using your products/services will solve those problems. Approach the conversation with one question in mind: "Who would lose the most or be inconvenienced the most if they buy from us?"

- Do the buyers fully understand your case studies, and did you explain them thoroughly? If not, is there a way to resend the case studies? Remember, it is your documented stories that are your most valid sales tools.

#4. If you identify something you missed, or you have a good idea what their objection could be, get the necessary information to them right away. Try to schedule another meeting with key members of the buyer's table. Use your skills of persuasion to express the importance of meeting with them again. Tell them that the information you have is imperative and could help in their ability to make the best decision.

When you go back in, present something relevant, and make sure you handle what you think could be their real objection. Don't be shy about asking direct questions and expecting answers: "You told us that you had a problem, and we have discovered and shown you exactly how we can help you can solve that problem. We've even shown you the benefits that you're going to be receiving as a result of working with us in solving that problem. What's really stopping you? What's really holding this up and how can I help?"

If you can't get a meeting, try to schedule a call to handle their potential concerns over the phone. If all else fails, the last resort is to email the information.

I strongly suggest you prepare yourself to move on to other big game. If you lose the deal and the loss lingers in your head and replays over and over again, it's robbing you of your time and the ambition to go out to find more good clients. No matter how good you are, you are going to lose some deals. It happens.

KNOW WHEN TO WALK AWAY

When you're hunting mid-sized and large sized opportunities, sometimes these complex deals take more time. The solution is patience, discipline, and ongoing proactive follow-up. Continually review your SWAP profile and look for other ways back in.

After you've done everything you can to get a stalled deal unstuck, you have to make some difficult decisions: when to and whether to walk away.

There's always danger in giving up. The deal could be

on hold for reasons way beyond your control, such as a spending freeze ordered by corporate, a merger or buyout, or a number of other disruptions. That's just part of doing business. Any time you give up without knowing that the deal is either off the table permanently or it went to a competitor, it's a big risk. You have to decide if you're going to wallow in negativity or move on to your other ideal prospects.

Even if you lose the deal, NEVER lose the lessons learned.

KEEP THE DOOR OPEN

Perhaps your competitor won the deal this time; there's a chance they still might not deliver on their promises. If the transition doesn't go well, or their product doesn't meet expectations, or if their salesperson oversold their capabilities, they may get tossed out of the account. Then you are back in the running, as long as you've maintained professionalism and good rapport with your contacts at the buyer's table.

If you lose a big deal, reach out with a gesture of professionalism and courtesy. Send a handwritten note or an email, stating, "Thank you for the opportunity to earn your business. We appreciate and respect your decision but want to make sure that you know that if everything's not perfect, we are here and happy to help. Let's stay in touch."

No matter what, always be gracious and professional, even if you feel the client was unkind to you or unfair in some way. When you take the high road, the door remains open, and you leave a chance to get back in available.

In the meantime, find creative ways to stay in contact with the buyer. You can put them on your company newsletter mailing list, add them to your email distribution list, or call them every sixty to ninety days to check in and see how things are going. Make sure you are connected on LinkedIn. You can also share new products with them or tell them about new updates at your company. If you lose a deal, that doesn't mean it's lost forever. When you're hunting big game, you have to take a long-term view. It's a marathon, not a sprint. Big deals are well worth the time and energy involved in executing a long-term strategy.

CHAPTER 12

RETENTION – A STRATEGY OF ITS OWN

To keep an account long-term, you have to constantly remind them of the value you have given them. Never assume they remember the value you have given them.

Much of this book focuses on the important task of hunting and winning new business. If your company is in growth mode, then you have to hunt new business. Often, one thing that gets overlooked in the hunt for new business is implementing an effective strategy to *keep* and *maintain* the accounts that you've worked so hard to win. This is critically important. Research shows that it takes just as much time and effort to *keep* your accounts as it does to *win* new accounts.

THE RAD TIME BLOCKING SYSTEM

You need a clearly defined process for maintaining all your existing customers, all while you still hunt, and you still grow your existing accounts. This is a lot to juggle and requires you to be very attentive to how you manage your time.

To stay on top of hunting, keeping, and growing your accounts, I've developed the **RAD** time management system. No, this is not a California surfer's time management method; this is exactly what top performers in almost all cases do.

Top Performers use "Time Blocking" strategies to make sure they can effectively juggle their selling hours in the most productive way. Depending on your territory, you will have to decide on how many hours you spend in each category. But, make no bones about it, you need to be effective at all three of these key areas. Too much imbalance (ie: only farming, and not hunting) can and will cause you to miss your numbers and impact your overall income.

The R stands for *retention*. This means you must block off set times for retaining and managing your existing accounts. Your objective in retention is not just to do what you told the client you were going to do. Your objective is to provide *more value* than they ever dreamed necessary. But you have to understand one element: keeping existing accounts is the easiest road you can take, but growing your territory takes more effort.

The A stands for *acquisition*. Acquisition involves scheduling set times for prospecting and acquiring new customers. Because of all the other tasks and obligations a salesperson has, very few reps spend time on new customer acquisition every week. Prospecting is one of the least enjoyable and most difficult parts of sales. Yet, top performers have blocks of time marked off every week when they get into proactive mode. It might be two hours on a Tuesday, three hours on a Friday. But you've got to commit to blocking that time solely for proactive activities. If you aren't actively scheduling acquisition time on your calendars every week, it simply won't get done. As Mike Weinberg, author of another great sales book says, "Nobody defaults to prospecting mode."

The D stands for account *development*. This is the third chunk of time to block off every week. Simply put, development means leveraging your existing customers to sell more to them. You already have a relationship with them, so you should be strategically looking for ways to sell them additional products and services—keeping in mind that the point is to make their process easier and their lives better. Account development rarely happens by accident. It takes strategy and planning, which you must schedule on your calendar.

Each week, salespeople who want to be top performers should spend 60 percent of their time on RAD activities, yet most don't. When I consult with companies and I'm meeting with one of their underperforming salespeople, I often ask to see their calendar. Usually, the only items on the calendar are set appointments and sales meetings. Seventy percent of the calendar is blank. If you want to raise the level of your income and success from average to top performer, the secret may well lie in your calendar.

MAINTENANCE STRATEGIES

On top of the RAD system, here are some strategies that will help you create beneficial habits for maintaining your accounts.

THE PARETO PRINCIPLE IN EFFECT

The Pareto Principle is also known as the 80/20 rule. As we discussed earlier in this book, if you create a spreadsheet of all your existing accounts and rank them by revenue and profit, you will likely see the Pareto Principle in full effect. Usually, the top 20 percent of your clients make up around 80 percent of your revenue and profitability. It's essential that you have a workable, repeatable, consistent strategy to maintain and retain existing accounts, especially for your top revenue producers. It is rare that you can effectively get to every single account you have, so you have to make sure you are investing your time in the wisest manner.

HOW TO KEEP YOUR COMPETITION OUT

A bona fide retention strategy goes way beyond just fulfilling your contract provisions, shipping your products, delivering on time, and staying within the planned budget. That's expected—and in your mind, it must be the bare minimum expectation. If you are striving to achieve service level agreements to maintain your accounts, then you are vulnerable to a competitor making inroads and stealing your accounts.

In this case, good enough is **not** enough. You have to offer additional value. Think in terms of what else you can do for your clients. Can you:

- Educate them about changes in the industry, new regulations, or shifts in the landscape of their business?
- See and inform them of issues, trends, and challenges they might be interested in?
- Advise them in certain areas where you have expertise?
- Provide them with important market data to help them make decisions?
- Show them product road maps?
- Invite them to company webinars?
- Bring in other experts or specialists at your company to teach the client something valuable?

- Go onsite with your clients and provide educational "lunch and learns"?

The more of these specialized activities you can present to your existing clients, the more value you provide. You will become a trusted partner. You want them to realize that if they ever lose you, then they will be losing a valuable resource that has implications for their long-term success. This helps you build a wall that keeps competitors out.

In fact, early in my career, I remember an executive saying in a meeting "Heck, we see Gene more than our current account rep from Compaq!" Long story short, I eventually won that deal because I showed up more, even when I didn't have the business.

THERE *IS* POWER IN PLANNED PARANOIA

I'm always slightly paranoid about losing my big accounts, especially the top 20 percent that generates most of my and my company's income. This mindset acts as my central motivation to plan and execute highly effective account retention activities.

The fact is that right now, as you're reading this book, your competitors are plotting and scheming on how they're going to take your best customers away from you. Your top accounts are on *some other* rep's target list—and that rep is going to aggressively pursue *your* accounts, the same ones you worked so hard to get. They're searching LinkedIn for a contact or a way in. They're likely sending over pricing way below yours. If you're not executing a proactive account retention strategy, you're vulnerable to losing business.

Keep those facts in mind every day and use them to drive the planning of your schedule and daily activities. Your clients need to have you at their forefront as much as you have them as your point of focus. A little healthy paranoia will prime you to actively implement the strategies I've taught in this book.

INTERVIEW WITH A BUYER

The best relationships are when the supplier and we agree on the strategic plan, that plan gets communicated to the entire team, the team is involved, and everyone is on the same page.

—SCOTT L., VP NORTH AMERICA, STRATEGIC SOURCING

BUILD YOUR ACCOUNT RETENTION STRATEGY WITH ONGOING VALUE

Take steps to creating a strategy that will keep your accounts from leaving you, by creating ongoing value. Ongoing value is defined as "what you do *after* you have won the opportunity."

Step #1. Ensure you have a flawless onboarding strategy when you first win the account. Don't let your relationship start off on the wrong foot by screwing up the transition. The most common reason the onboarding process fails is not due to process, but miscommunication. Make sure you are on top of the onboarding process. Confirm that your people are connected with and talking to their people. There is nothing worse than a poor initial onboarding experience. Start off on the right foot by making sure all the dots are connected, that your team is hitting their deadlines, and stay on this until the delivery of the products and services are complete. Do not leave this to chance. And always remembers Murphy's Law—"anything that can go wrong, will go wrong."

Step #2. Once the deal is closed, become the quarterback and supervisor of the integration process. This will help avoid hiccups in the switchover from the previous vendor to your company. Equally important, your oversight of the integration will help the client realize that you are not just a sales person who swoops in to close the sale—you're committed to *ensuring their success*. You can build tremendous rapport and a relationship of trust with the new client if you are onsite and proactive during the onboarding process.

The best sellers are fanatical about their client's success.

Step #3. Have a predetermined, systematic process mapped out in advance. The best way to effectively quarterback the transition is to make sure your plan is solid but also flexible enough to allow custom changes for the client's unique needs. A set process will help make sure nothing slips through the cracks, and no balls are dropped.

Step #4. Make sure everyone who will be affected by the transition has 24-hour contact information. I'm not talking about the main customer service line here. They need to know they can contact you, the VP, and the local supervisor if they have any needs or concerns. Make sure they call you if there is any problem. In a worst-case scenario, your client calls to report a mess up, they get some random person in the company to address the issue, the situation is never reported to you, and then the blockers at the client's company run around saying, "I told you so." You have to be on top of every detail during this critical phase.

Step #5. Have predetermined checkpoints identified in the process and discuss each with the client to make sure they are satisfied. This is your chance to strengthen your reputation as an essential success partner. Don't let a shoddy, disorganized integration process ruin your relationship with the client. Be their point of security, acting as an advocate at every step. I recommend that you schedule regular calls with your key contacts during the transition so that you are on top of every detail. Do not leave this to chance.

REMIND THE CLIENT OF YOUR VALUE

Another important concept in account retention is to track your success and publicize your wins. Now that your products or services are implemented within your new client company, you want to constantly promote the fact that they've made a good decision. The best way to do this is to have frequent and ongoing check-ins with them to discuss how it's going.

Look for factual data points that prove it was a good decision: is the line running faster, better, less expensive, smoother? Have you heard specific comments from employees of the company? Document every win, even create a chart or infographic that demonstrates the success if it makes sense. Then, broadcast it to everyone at the company, emailing all your decision makers so that they are aware of the success in their decision to choose you and your company. This is a habit you should develop and continue long-term *because clients have short memories*, quickly forgetting wins, positive change, and breakthroughs that you created for them three months ago.

Reminder: Clients tend to have short-term memories; make sure you remind them of all the progress you have made with them. Remind them of all the great things that have happened since deciding on you and your company.

Soon you'll have a list of wins to share in an account review. This way, your account review is more than just the X's and O's of what you have done—it spends more time talking about the value they and their team are experiencing because of working with you.

If you can't get a meeting for a live account review, you can always use a year-end email or one-year anniversary email to everyone at the buyer's table. Make sure you are keeping track of these wins. In today's busy world, most people can't remember what they were even doing two months ago, let alone what you have done for them. Remind them.

STRIVE FOR CONTINUOUS IMPROVEMENT

Constantly ask yourself, "What else could I be doing *even better* for my client?" Commit to always doing more than what you said you would. Avoid committing to more than you can deliver on. In sales, the old adage holds true, "under-promise and over-deliver"—never the other way around. Yet I still see this today. Big mistake.

Under-promising and over-delivering creates impressive wins for you to share with your client. When you do more than you say you would do, you exceed the scope of the deal, surpass expectations, and ultimately, you strengthen your bond.

Continually seek feedback on every level of service you provide. Ask questions like, "Is everything going great? Are we exceeding your expectations? What could we do *even* better?" Notice I said "*even* better." That's very different from, "What could we do better?"

Making that distinction changes your question from implying something isn't going well to looking for ways to excel beyond your current excellence.

The fact is, they can always find somebody cheaper. There's always some other company knocking on their door offering a lower price. You have to pull yourself out of the price-quality-service conversation and place yourself firmly in the realm of valued partner status. Valued partners are very hard to find, and even harder to replace, if you are doing everything I have discussed so far.

THE STRATEGIC ACCOUNT REVIEW

Conducting quarterly or bi-annual account reviews is an essential strategy in client retention. An account review is a scheduled, face-to-face meeting with key members of the buyer's table to evaluate your performance as a supplier/vendor/partner/firm.

Its importance cannot be overstated.

Here's why:

#1. There's no better time than face time. The account review is a tremendous opportunity to meet face-to-face with senior executives and members of the buyer's table. When you are in front of these people, you can see their faces, read their body language, and determine their level of satisfaction—whether they're happy with your service or product or not.

#2. Review all the work you've completed thus far. In essence, this is a chance to show them what a great job you've been doing—how many units you've shipped, what percentage was on time, what the failure rate was, and so on. Again, clients have short term memories. Reminding them of all the ways you've helped them is a legitimate strategy.

#3. Confirm that everything is on track and going well. Remind them that you've done everything you said you would do and help them reaffirm that they made a good decision. Ask them, "Is everything on track in your opinion? Have we delivered on everything we promised?"

#4. If the answer to the question in #3 is no, then you can find out exactly why the client is dissatisfied and correct it. Maybe they've had some complaints from the shipping department. Maybe the pallets are breaking, or the plastic wrap is too hard to remove. Minor annoyances can add up to big problems with customer satisfaction over time. This is your chance to uncover any problems and solve them. When you come across a problem, you must work immediately to rectify it. Call whomever you need to within your company, keeping the client updated on your progress in solving their issue.

#5. Remind the client of all the work you've done above and beyond what is specified in the contract. This is another point I cannot overstate. Remind them of how many of their employees attended your training and your webinars. Remind them how you helped streamline their delivery process. Remind them how you advised them on decisions and brought them industry intelligence and data. I've found that key decision makers high up in the organization don't often know about any of the extra work you've been doing. Account reviews give you a chance to impress the executives.

Top performing salespeople are not just in the business of getting new clients, they're also in the repeat and ongoing business. This is built into a strategic client retention strategy.

#6. The most valuable benefits of conducting account reviews are referrals! Asking your existing clients for referrals—to both other divisions within their own company and outside companies—is something every top performer does. Yet 95 percent of *all* salespeople fail to or forget to ask.

There's a little-known secret to successfully mining referrals.

In a word, it's all about your *timing*.

If you are committed to asking, when is the best time to ask?

When the sale is made? No.

After the first delivery? No again.

Before you ask for any referrals, you have to prime your client into a "referral giving" mindset. How do you do this? Read on.

A well done account review will put them in this state of mind. You've just presented that you've done what you said you would do and even more: you've helped their company strive further toward their goals, you've confirmed that everything is on track, and you've asked about problems and shown a commitment to fixing them. You've reminded them of your above and beyond commitment to the contract requirement and shown them that you are a good partner in their success.

Now is the time to ask for referrals.

If the time is right, there are best practices for asking for a referral. Approach your client with confidence and certainty, and say, "I'm curious. I've been trying to meet with Steve over in the other building. Do you know Steve? Would you mind sending him a note or even calling him and giving me an introduction?"

Now, if you've done everything else right, the odds are that someone will gladly call Steve and give you that warm introduction and speed you through the process. You can also ask for referrals to other companies, referrals to other buying units within this company that aren't buying from you, or referrals to other people in the company whom you haven't been able to meet. Remember, the additional benefit to a well done account review is that you are inducing people into what Business Growth Expert Scott Hallman calls a "peak referral state."

When you ask for referrals, don't just ask them for the contact information of the person to whom they're referring you. Ask for a personal introduction. Ask them to include in their referral the excellent job you've done for them, and that they made a good decision choosing you. Remember, top performing salespeople are not just in the getting new clients business, they're also in the repeat and referral business. That's built into their strategic client retention strategy.

TIPS FOR HOLDING AN EFFECTIVE ACCOUNT REVIEW

Send an agenda to all attendees in advance.

In your presentation, include the following slides:

- Identify the work you've done so far (include numbers, dates, and details. But don't overdo it)
- What you learned during this process
- Key successes (quantified benefits are preferred)
- Issues you identified for the client and how you resolved them (be specific)
- Confirmation that everything is on track (ask them)
- How else can you help them?
- How can you be even better?

THE IMMENSE POWER OF ONGOING TEACHING AND EDUCATING

This point is worth repeating because it is a highly effective tool in adding value and providing excellent service for your client: don't underestimate the power of offering teaching and training sessions to your clients. What do they need to learn that you can provide? It doesn't have to be content developed by your company. You can repurpose articles about their business, industry, or marketplace. Are there any new rules or regulations they need to know about? The trainings don't have to be live, although that is preferred. You can use webinars if the location is geographically far from you. Webinars are the next best thing (and a heck of a lot less expensive) than live training. If you have not mastered Webinar-based training, I highly recommend that you jump in the water and learn this technology. In fact, I *rarely* converse with a client without some type of visual aid.

One of my favorite things to do as part of client retention is called "Lunch and Learns." Everybody loves free food, right? During a Lunch and Learn, I bring in lunch, and while they eat I present an educational topic related to their business. I try to keep a casual and interactive atmosphere with plenty of questions from the audience. Lunch and Learns also provide face time with actual users of your product or service. Invite the supervisors, managers, and even the line workers who use your products on a daily basis. These are often the people who know your product the best. They can give you very important feedback, including positive testimonials, as well as identify problems or challenges. Remember, you are in this for the long haul; pay special attention to the people that are actually using your product or service.

Do not overlook the necessity and benefits of an organized and proactive account retention strategy. The more value you provide to the client, the harder it will be for a competitor to replace you and steal your business. And believe me, they are trying.

Now that we've discussed *hunting* and *keeping* business, let's dive into every company's hidden gold mine—growing the accounts you already have.

CHAPTER 13

CAPTURING LOW HANGING FRUIT

Most companies have a gold mine within their existing accounts. Yet few companies fully execute the solution sell.

—GENE MCNAUGHTON

One of the easiest ways to grow your revenue is to go after low-hanging fruit by expanding your sales with existing accounts. One of the top sales producers in one of our accounts said, "I land 'em, then I expand 'em."

If you've completed the activities in the previous chapter and executed an effective account retention plan, by now your clients will view you as a trusted resource and success partner. They likely will be open to doing more business with you. In fact, they might just seek you out on their own with offers to expand your company's role. These offers usually come in the form of the following questions: "Does your company provide this service? Can your company help us with this? We're looking for a new provider in this area, do you know anything about that?" Learn to recognize these as buying questions; they indicate a need that your client has and that you may be able to fill.

KILLER METHODS FOR SELLING MORE WITHIN

More often than not, opportunities to sell more to an existing client won't fall in your lap, so you'll want to take action on the best methodologies for the job. This means you'll need a preplanned, consistent strategy to grow your existing accounts.

The first strategy is to commit to the *upsell*. This refers to selling your clients a more expensive product, or just a greater amount of the same product. For example, you may have a premium product line that you can upsell your accounts on using, instead of the standard product line they're using currently. Or maybe you have a contract to provide half of the client's total product needs, while one of your competitors provides the other half. You can maneuver to upsell to the point where you are providing 75 percent of the business. That is, as long as you and your company perform beyond your client's (or competitor's) expectations. Again, this is why consistent and highly effective account reviews are so powerful.

Often companies engage with me for a keynote speech, or two-day sales Bootcamp. Over the course of time, they become full service consulting clients, with me and my team joining them to build out their entire sales playbook, orchestrate their CRM (usually Salesforce.com), creating their reports, and working with marketing to create their case studies, white papers, presentations, and webinars. Now that, my friends, is what the upsell is all about—establishing deep relationships and finding additional ways to help the greater good of the client company.

A second strategy to develop an account is to cross-sell them on other product lines your company provides. For example, if you got into the account by selling your safety harnesses and fall protection products, once you've earned their trust, you can try to sell them on your fire protection product lines. Your success in upselling and cross-selling will depend on your performing timely account reviews, getting face time with key decision makers, and being seen as a trusted partner.

A third strategy is to look for business opportunities in other divisions of the same company. These could be other geographical locations, or entirely different business units. For example, if you're selling access systems to the aircraft manufacturing division of a large conglomerate, you might find great success by also selling to their aerospace division. Distinct business units within large companies often operate totally independently. If you leverage your referral properly, you may be able to develop that account and double or triple your total revenue. The key is leveraging the success of your existing business to gain entryway or access to other divisions. We do this regularly with our larger, global accounts. In other words, we perform far beyond expectation, we conduct our account reviews (reminding them of everything we helped them do over our year-long relationship) and ask about key leaders from other organizations within that same company. In one Global Security company, we have worked with five different divisions! Remember, in the global companies, most of the regions and sometimes even product lines act as if they are their own company. Never assume that they are talking. The bigger the company usually means less cross functional communication.

A fourth strategy to develop your accounts is to incentivize them to place larger orders in exchange for bulk discounts. For example, if they typically buy a three-month supply, offer them a discount for buying a one-year supply up front. Or, if you sold X amount of your products to a client in their last order, offer them a 10 percent discount if they can commit to buying two times the amount of product in their next order. Ten percent of a large order represents a substantial savings. This offer might generate a response like, "Well, our satellite offices also use this product, so if we centralize our purchases and buy it all from you, that would save us a fortune."

In other words, if you always have your client's best interest in mind, and you show them how to be an even better buyer of your products, they tend to stay with you for a long time.

LEVERAGE THE ACCOUNT REVIEW PROCESS

The best way to develop an account is to leverage your account review process. Here's an example: I was engaged to help a large accounting firm with forty offices. They were having huge struggles in winning new business and were spending no time hunting the big deals that were in their office areas. Instead of starting out with all forty offices, we agreed to try a six-month pilot program in just six of the offices. No problem. During that six months, I worked hard to track successes and record and quantify the big wins that they achieved during this tenure. I am not saying we were the reason they won these deals (they are really great at what they do) but I can tell you that they weren't winning them before we got there.

At the end of the six months, I did a full account review with all their decision-making partners. I went through the account review slides (laid out earlier in this book) and talked about the big wins and successes of the pilot program. I included numbers to quantify the success and showed them some of the problems we encountered, as well as how we overcame them. Then I said, "Now, what would happen if we were able to expand the pilot program, and your other thirty-four offices all achieved the same benefits and successes that we had in the pilot?"

Needless to say, we developed that account from just six locations to a total of forty through the power of the account review. Over the five years that we worked together, this accounting firm went from not even using the word "sales" to becoming a well-oiled machine, with recorded online training courses, regular live training, and a detailed New Partner Sales training program. Very few consulting firms can tout that they keep and expand their services to clients for more than five years. For us, that is not unusual.

Bottom line, if you continue to hunt for additional ways

to add more value, you will usually find it. Where your focus goes, your energy will flow.

> The best way to develop an account is to leverage your account review process. As soon as they are happily impressed by your relationship, they are more open for you to ask about other areas or products they may want to hear more about.

The takeaway is that when your clients are happy, and you show them the good work you've been doing for them via an account review, it allows you to ask for more business and for referrals. It also allows you to suggest other solutions that they may not be thinking about. A thorough account review helps you get the low-hanging fruit and puts the decision makers in a peak referral mindset.

THE ACCOUNT DEVELOPMENT PROFILE

Another consistent habit of top performers is that they build an account development profile document for each of their major accounts. It is an extension of the SWAP profile, but it specifically focuses on the best way to grow their revenue within each account. This is called an *account development strategy*.

The account development strategy is a road map of the additional products you plan to sell to an account and how you plan to do it. It lists the other divisions or business units of an account that could become buyers, as well as their key decision makers and their decision process. A good account strategy helps identify the potential of each account and prioritize your development activities.

THE FIVE KEYS TO DEVELOPING YOUR ACCOUNTS

Account development helps you grow your business faster and easier than focusing all your time and energy on hunting new accounts. *Do not miss this opportunity.* Make sure you're hitting all five of the key elements of growing your business:

#1. **Have a preplanned strategy**. Every great account developer I've worked with knows in advance what else they could be selling to a client. Then they develop a plan of attack to go after that business by leveraging their existing success within that account.

#2. **Strive to continuously maximize your face time with decision makers.** The more you are on site at the client's location, the more connections you can build and strengthen. Combine this with building value for the client when you are on site and soon you will be a trusted partner. *There is no better time than facetime.*

#3. **Continue to build strong connections.** Stay in touch

with all the people you met with when you first won the account. Rely on them for information and referrals, and always work to forge new connections with decision makers in other areas. The fastest way to get a meeting with anyone is through a warm referral from somebody they trust.

#5. Focus on creating ongoing value. As you build up your reputation as a knowledgeable resource and success partner, use that reputation to add value in other areas of the company. Continue offering education and training. Use LinkedIn to share articles, trending reports, awards that your company has won, and key industry news.

#5. Bring in the right team at the right time. If the customer is having a technical product issue, bring in one of your engineers. If it's a shipping problem, bring in a logistics expert. Bottom line, you've heard me talk about team-based selling, right? Well this is the same approach. You do not have to know everything about everything, but you do need to know who your internal company experts are and bring them in when necessary.

PITFALLS TO AVOID IN ACCOUNT DEVELOPMENT

Never assume your client has gone to your website to see every-thing you offer—this rarely happens. You have to be proactive in bringing up additional products and services.

Mistake #1. Don't act like a salesperson who is just sniffing for commissions. Many salespeople don't bother visiting their existing accounts unless they have a new product to sell or they want something. Customers can and will sense that, and if they think you only visit them when you want to sell them something, they will stop taking your meetings.

You have to make sure that you have plenty of face time with your accounts, preferably onsite, and that you are conducting prescheduled account reviews. Verify that the client is happy and ask what else you can do for them. You have to do your retention work before you can do your development work. Don't disappear for six months and then show up only when you want to make another sale.

Mistake #2. Never suggestive sell without a reason. You have to think this through in advance so that your development activities are logical and make sense to the buyer. If you haven't thought it through in advance, you won't be confident in explaining why they need what you are teeing up and ultimately, you're recommending. If the customer senses you are just trying to upsell them to make more commission, you are in big trouble. In fact, doing that is uncomfortable for both you and the buyer.

Mistake #3. Having only one key contact in a company. This is too risky. Yet, I see it all the time. What if that person leaves the company? Well, then you are back to square one, trying to get a meeting with the new decision maker. Or worse, you get bounced downstairs to procurement. Then you are vulnerable to the competition. You should always work hard to develop and maintain relationships with multiple decision makers at every key account.

Mistake #4. Assuming your customers know about every product and service you offer. As salespeople, we know our product lines so well we assume that our customers must also know about them too. Not true. Your customers are rarely going to your website to study your product and service set, nor your company. They don't have time. Don't expect them to come to you when they have a need in another area outside of what you are providing them right now. It's your job to develop that account and uncover other needs that you can fill for them.

A partner in my accounting client firm told me one time, "I was onsite with our client, and while I was there I saw one of my competitors, of whom I had known for several years. I asked the client why my competitor was there. He said that they were working on a specialized consulting project. I asked him why he didn't ask me to be part of that.

"He said, 'Because I didn't know you did that. Otherwise we would have had you do it.'"

Good lesson learned. Don't let this be you.

Mistake #5. Expecting that an existing customer is naturally going to give you a referral. This rarely happens. You have to work hard for referrals and ask for them at the right time—and only after you've earned the right by offering far more value than they expected.

Remember the intrinsic value of account development: it means more revenue and more sales with less effort. You're already in the account and, if you're implementing the strategies in this book, providing excellent service, additional sales will be much easier. I can't emphasize enough the importance of a predefined, managed process for account development. If you follow the process I've laid out, you will greatly increase the revenue you're generating in the accounts you already have.

Is it easy? No.

Is it worth it? Absolutely.

"The strategist always beats the tactician."

—CHET HOLMES, AUTHOR OF *THE ULTIMATE SALES MACHINE*

CONCLUSION

Thank you for trusting me enough to invest your time into reading this book. Being an avid reader, I know that today more than ever, it is hard to squeeze more time in a day to read (or listen to) an entire book.

If you did that, I congratulate you. And I am grateful for you.

I started this book journey almost ten years ago. I would start, then get busy and stop. I would start again, a life change would happen, and I would stop again. But, I never quit. I refused, even when some people told me it would never happen.

Instead of trying to squeeze in a few minutes each day, between a busy travel schedule, client meetings/calls/

webinars, coaching my son's sports teams, and life in general I put my trust in Tucker Max and his team at Book in a Box. By spending some money, I was able to work with an entire team, including writers, designers, consultants, marketers, and ultimately publishing. What you are holding in your hands is ten years of hearing "So when is that book coming out?" and battling the demons of the naysayers.

I am more than proud of this, purely for the fact that it is yet another time in my life when I became so committed to something, I visualized it, I really focused on it, and then, it became reality.

And frankly, I could tell you hundreds of other stories just like that. I got clear on what I wanted, I established the main reasons why I wanted it, and I took massive action to achieve it. When I hit a roadblock, I exercised all my resources to find a team of experts to help me achieve the outcome. And in your hands (or ears if you are listening) is the proof that this simple formula works.

I have learned that we cannot grow without the positive intervention of another human being.

So, what about you?

What do you really want out of your sales or sales leadership career? What does success look like to you? What does it *mean* to you? And more importantly, what will it feel like after you have achieved that success?

How about being able to positively serve more people?

What about making even more income?

What about being an amazing role model for your family and kids?

And then there's that feeling of being able to positively impact the lives of other people around you. How does that feel when you contribute to others?

In my answers to all the questions above, it helps me realize, even more, why I love having a career in sales. This is one of the few careers where we truly are in control of our own destiny.

And here is what's crucial to understand: the better you get at this craft, the more impact you can have in all the areas that I named above.

And know this, I'm just a kid from a small town in Iowa, right in the middle of the United States. If I can learn and do this stuff, you can too.

But, you have to do the work.

Where do you go from here?

First, as I have mentioned throughout the book, I have a whole toolkit of free resources for you to download and put into action.

If you haven't yet, go to www.salesedgetoolkit.com. On this page, I include many of the same workshops and worksheets that I use with my clients. Those are yours to use for free.

Some of you may want to go further. I get it. Reading (or listening to) a book is one thing, but how do you get access to this valuable information and experience the repetition that is needed to continue to pursue mastery? One way is through online video-based training. If you go to www.theultimatesalesmasterysystem.com you will find a host of video-based training programs, some of which are free. If you choose to unlock the entire system, it is very affordable for you and your team to get USMS Certified. This not only looks good on your resume, but more importantly, it will serve up, in shorter digestible chunks, the best of the best of what I have learned in over thirty-two years of selling.

For those of you who want and need coaching—someone to work with you directly, who is highly trained on the skillsets from this book, as well as being a tenured business leader who now is in a coaching career—go to www.salesedgetoolkit.com to learn more. Look, every top performer in any profession has a coach. This is not just an expert at the skillset, but someone who is trained to be your accountability coach to help you to follow through on the actions you need to take to create the career and life of your dreams. We have expert coaches who can give you one-on-one attention to help speed up your process of success.

And finally, for bigger companies, we have our Consulting Division. This division is designed with a team of expert resources who will come in and do most of the work for you. From designing your compensation programs, your hiring processes, your sales process, training, marketing collateral—we have a wicked smart team of experts that we can deploy into your company and based off conducting our coveted Business Growth Audit (outlined in earlier chapters of this book), we will come in and give you a complete independent review of your business processes as they relate to sales, marketing, and customer service. We have performed this intense audit for well over 100 companies and consistently build and deliver world class growth plans and have proven to help companies shatter sales records.

If you want to stop trying to reinvent the wheel, or you keep doing the same things over and over while expecting different results (and not getting them) we have resources that have proven to help people just like you to achieve monumental heights.

And finally, to you, the reader—thank you again for reading this book. You are now in the category of the "few who do, vs. those that talk about it." Great job.

Now, grab your online tools, roll up your sleeves, and get to work.

The future is an awesome force.

Know that you will always be rewarded in public for the things you practice in private. Work hard on yourself, invest in yourself, stay focused on your targets, and the sky is the limit!

Peace and Love,

Gene

ABOUT THE AUTHOR

 Regarded as one of the nation's most effective business growth experts, **GENE McNAUGHTON** has spent more than 25 years generating top results for Fortune 500 companies, including helping grow Gateway Computers from a small company to an $11 billion international powerhouse. A consultant, public speaker, and sales trainer, Gene McNaughton created a path for new sales techniques and expert methods of influence, and he challenges his audiences to travel confidently with him on that path.

Made in the USA
Coppell, TX
18 November 2019